Willing • Available • Ready •

RÉGINE MFOUMOU

Willing • Available • Ready •
to live

Rhema Publications
London, United Kingdom

DEDICATION

To all believers of Christ.

ACKNOWLEDGEMENTS

First, I want to thank the Lord for His ever-present love and strength that brought me to where I am today. Indeed, without Him, I can do absolutely nothing: thank you Jesus, my passion and my life are all devoted to You.

I also want to thank my children, Jules-Aurélien Arthur and Bertrand Arthur, for their unwavering and discreet support: even when you have to share me with so many people at church or when I travel around the world, you have never given reasons to worry. You are truly my greatest blessing from God! May God bless you abundantly and always keep you and give you everything you desire. I love you.

Thank you to Pastor Svein Berge and his lovely wife, Greta Berge. You are an answered prayer. I learn so much with you. I love you. God bless you.

Thank you to my brothers and sisters at Rhema Resource Centre in London, Haiti and Cameroon: your renewed support gives me the strength to pursue the vision that God has given me. I love you all. God bless you.

TABLE OF CONTENTS

Chapter VI

Keys to Success in War **105**

Chapter VII

The Mystery of the Upper Room **133**

Chapter VIII

Willing, Available, Ready? **137**

CONCLUSION **155**

FOREWORD

Pastor Regine Mfoumou is a true servant of God. She is the founder and leading minister of Rhema Resource Centre church. She is also the owner of Rhema Publications and the author of various books. And here she comes back with a new book!

In this book, she points straight to the problem. Her message is definitively a wake-up call to the body of Christ. It is indeed a challenge to every one of us to examine ourselves in the light of God's Word, take our relationship with God, our calling and responsibility that God has given us seriously.

God has given her a burden and a calling: to get us all to stand up and shake off our laziness, love for comfort, our lack of discipline and our slumbering, as we consecrate and commit ourselves fully to the Lord Himself as well as to His work. Her words in this book are sharp and straight to the point.

Pastor Regine doesn't just point to the problem, but she also points to the solution. The same, she doesn't just set the diagnosis, but she also gives us the medicine, the remedy for the situation.

You want to find out what the solution is? Well, then you need to get into the book: read it and find out personally what is the strongly needed solution provided us from the Lord. But one thing we can say is this: this is fiery preaching and Bible-based teaching that takes us out of our fantasy world straight into revelation knowledge. Be of good cheer and enjoy your reading of the book.

Svein Berge,

Pastor/Bible teacher.

INTRODUCTION

Almost every believer of Christ has this pat answer, ready to be tossed out like a bullet when challenged, questioned or simply asked about their belief: 'I have faith!' Yes, indeed, we all have faith. We all believe that God has brought us far from the dryness and wilderness of this fallen world to a better place through His Son Jesus. Yes, faith is the nerve of war we need to battle the enemy. Nevertheless, many sons and daughters of God seem to lack active faith and struggle for the things already restored to them through Christ. To aggravate this is the fact that many local churches focus on teachings that are grounded in humanism instead of the throne of grace. This gives ample opportunity for the enemy to confuse, delay and sometimes divert us from our goal. So, instead of displaying that we are more than conquerors in Christ Jesus, we are adding to the ranks of unprepared spiritual soldiers rather than raising solid believers who can stand on their spiritual ground.

Today, many people have head knowledge of the Word of God because they read the Bible every day or go to church regularly. But they also mistakenly believe that doing so means they have faith in God. The truth is that the mainsprings of our faith stem from God, who entrusts us with the gifts of the Holy Spirit in order to fulfil His (not our) purposes in us and through us:

...to each one the manifestation of the Spirit is given for the common good. To one there is given through the Spirit a message of wisdom, to another a message of knowledge by means of the same Spirit, to another faith by the same Spirit, to another gifts of healing by that one Spirit, to another miraculous powers, to another prophecy, to another distinguishing between spirits, to another speaking in different kinds of tongues, and to still another the interpretation of tongues (1 Corinthians 12:7-10).

In other words, God generously gives those who have accepted His Son faith in varying measures through the Holy Spirit, our Helper and Counsellor. It is He who is also available to teach us the things we do not know and help us remember the Word of God as it is written: *"...the Advocate, the Holy Spirit, whom the Father will send in my name, will teach you all things and will remind you of everything I have said to you" (John 14:26).* When, then, has the Holy Spirit become a messenger we can send out to fight evildoers or our persecutors, when the Word of God says, *"love your enemies and pray for those who persecute you" (Matthew 5:44)?* When has the Spirit of God become the gossip who gives messages to spread strife, suspicion or confusion among the people of God? Unfortunately, some well-intentioned, but spiritually weak individuals have been led astray to hate or become suspicious of family members, friends, loved ones and so on through a 'prophetic word'.

Now, we also know that the Word reminds us of the truth concerning our faith. Although some believers tend to deny it, yet it remains the truth:

> *...Because you have so little faith. Truly I tell you, if you have faith as small as a mustard seed, you can say to this mountain, 'Move from here to there,' and it will move. Nothing will be impossible for you (Matthew 17:20).*

"...As small as a mustard seed!" A grain of mustard is about 1 to 2 millimetres (0.039 to 0.079 inches) in diameter. That, figuratively, is the size of the faith God is asking us to have to move the mountains stopping us from moving forward in life. Consequently, this brings about another inevitable question: why are so many believers living a yo-yo existence with more downs than ups while claiming to live in the victory in Christ?

Nowadays, we often hear about depression among Christians or people who confess Christ but are so burdened that it seems like all the mountains of the world have confined them. Is it not paradoxical, on the one hand, to always claim and proclaim that Jesus is the Lord of lords and the King of kings, while, on the other hand, feel completely overwhelmed by an unfulfilled and distressed life?

Another biblically misinterpreted truth is that Jesus never promised His followers a life free of problems or difficulties. On the contrary, He said: *"I have told you these things, so that in me you may have peace. In this world, you will have trouble. But take heart! I have overcome the world" (John 16:33).* Awareness of this truth is key to understanding how we can overcome the troubles of this world.

But, do we truly grasp the meaning of having victory in Christ? The plain fact about having a victory implies that a fight, an opposition or some adverse condition must first be present for that victory to take place. Forgetting this reality is what causes so much confusion in the minds of some believers, who still don't understand the necessity to fight to take the ground that Jesus has already won on the Cross for us. The Bible clearly states that *"Your enemy the devil prowls around like a roaring lion looking for someone to devour" (1 Peter 5:8).* So, the greatest lie anyone can ever tell themselves is that becoming a Christian will keep all their problems at bay. In fact, the good news is that, once you become a Christian, because of your shift from the world usurped by Satan (though he is not in control), you fundamentally become an adversary of the devil. He hates you because you belong to Christ. He hates the fact that you have a relationship he can never have with God. He hates your happiness; he hates your success; he hates your peace. And, because he knows the Word of God (logos), he will study you to know your weaknesses and use them against you. He will look for opportunities to tempt you just when you are the most vulnerable as he did with Jesus Himself in the wilderness (see Matthew 4:1-11).

However, God has provided the solution for us to be able to overcome the tricks, the snares, the lies and the arrows of the enemy. After warning us of the danger we are in, the Word says: *"Resist him, steadfast in the faith, knowing that the same sufferings are experienced by your brotherhood in the world" (1 Peter 5:9).* *"Resist,"* and what else do we need? *"Steadfast faith!"* Once again, faith is needed in the fight with our eyes set on the promises of victory in Christ, for He will fight our battles:

> *For the Lord your God is the one who goes with you*
> *to fight for you against your enemies to give you*
> *victory (Deuteronomy 20:4).*

And when the battle is too intense for us to bear, He promises to provide a means of escape:

> *No temptation has overtaken you except what is*
> *common to mankind. And God is faithful; he will not*
> *let you be tempted beyond what you can bear. But*
> *when you are tempted, he will also provide a way out*
> *so that you can endure it (1 Corinthians 10:13).*

The concept of faith has appeared several times so far in the discussion, so let's now look at a definition of faith. The Merriam Webster online definition provides five interesting meanings:

1. allegiance to duty or a person
2. fidelity to one's promises
3. belief and trust in and loyalty to God

4. a firm belief in something for which there is no proof

5. something that is believed especially with strong conviction

When someone says, 'I have faith,' what do they mean exactly? Let's be more precise by rephrasing the definitions above. When you say you have faith, which of the following apply to you?

1. You are acknowledging your allegiance to the Lord so as to live a life pleasing to Him.

2. You have been faithful in your walk with Him, showing fidelity to your promises to follow Him and serve Him.

3. You are expressing your belief, trust in and loyalty to God.

4. You have a firm belief that God will act in your life. No matter what is happening right now, you don't need to have proof to know that God will act anyway.

5. And, finally, you believe in God and God's actions and you are strongly convinced that He will do something about your situation.

Gathering these definition points together may give rise to questions many people have never asked themselves since giving their life to Jesus. Yet, several verses lead us to the same definitions:

> *Now faith is the substance of things hoped for, the evidence of things not seen (Hebrews 11:1).*

> *For we walk by faith, not by sight (2 Corinthians 5:7).*

...that your faith should not stand in the wisdom of men, but in the power of God (1 Corinthians 2:5).

For by grace are ye saved through faith; and that not of yourselves: it is the gift of God (Ephesians 2:8 KJV).

If all the above verses are undeniable truths, they should be demonstrated in every believer's walk with Christ.

Let's be very precise right here before moving forward: this book is not about faith in general, it is talking about *your* faith. Why? Because God answers the prayers of His faith-filled disciples... those who put their trust in Him! Our battles are won by faith: *"...take up the shield of faith, with which you can extinguish all the flaming arrows of the evil one"* (Ephesians 6:16). Therefore, having faith in God's might is the starting point of your victory.

The main purpose of this book, therefore, is to strengthen and uplift your spirit to stand up and fight back for what is yours. But we must fight in the way the Bible says we should. As you read through and reposition yourself spiritually, you will be able to tangibly experience victory instead of proclaiming it hypothetically. Victory in Christ is the portion of every believer who abides in Christ, and His Word abides in them: *"If you remain in me and my words remain in you, ask whatever you wish, and it will be done for you"* (John 15:7).

The second aim of this book is to remind every reader that the Spirit of God alone is the Revelator who can show us the truths that can help us become overcomers. He can guide us through our shortcomings, weaknesses and struggles, and help us to remain close to God, especially during hardships. As we investigate the way the Spirit of God guided Jesus towards His mission on earth, it is important to stress that every believer should learn to… pause! Yes! Pause… to reflect and meditate instead of moving forward aimlessly.

Christians cannot wander around on earth as if they have no purpose! When promising to establish the Church, Jesus said *"the gates of Hades will not overcome it" (Matthew 16:18)* and that He gives us *"the keys of the kingdom of heaven" (Matthew 16:19)*. This promise was fulfilled on the Day of Pentecost and the Church started experiencing the greater things Jesus had also told them (see John 14:12). Since then, the life-giving Spirit has been at work, leading people to repentance and to the knowledge of Christ, healing and delivering from evil spirits. The life in Christ must be visible because its light overshadows any form of darkness! Today, many believers of Christ are confused about their purpose and wonder how they can shape their desires and individual aspirations to live the abundant life offered to them through the Sacrifice of the Cross.

Unpretentious to provide exclusive answers to all questions, this book will enable everyone seeking direction, guidance or facing unanswered prayers and adverse situations to challenge themselves to a permanent change in their lives. *"Is anything too hard for the Lord?" (Genesis 18:14)*. We all know the answer! We all are willing to LIVE, to enjoy life and all that it offers. But are we always AVAILABLE and READY for what we hope for? Surely a part of us is. Hopefully, each chapter of this book will enable you to redirect your life, or at least certain areas of it, as it gradually unfolds methods used in biblical times as well as principles of God that helped people come through great struggles, doubts and persecutions that anyone of us may experience at this very moment.

The Word of God says, *"When you ask, you do not receive, because you ask with wrong motives, that you may spend what you get on your pleasures" (James 4:3)*. So, starting with the state and challenges of today's Church that may affect or influence our walk with the Lord, through the pages, you will be inspired, by God's grace, to ask yourselves the right questions. In this seeking mode, you will be able to renew your mind by making crucial decisions. You will be able to stand boldly before the throne of God to receive from Him what you have been asking Him for. Our God is faithful, generous, willing, available and ready to give always. In short, unless we know what to do and take appropriate biblical actions because we are willing, available and ready too, we cannot win the war against the enemy.

Chapter I
The Twenty-First Century Church

There is a deficient understanding of Christ today within the body of Christ itself, which has brought confusion in the minds of many believers. Very often, we hear people say we should 'leave things in the hands of God…', 'God will do it…', or 'God is in control'. But the sound of resignation behind such expressions is appalling enough to make us wonder what today's Church is teaching the believers.

When we look closely at the way the early Church functioned, it becomes obvious that today's postmodern Church is preaching a watered-down gospel. It has limited a great number of believers by depriving them of the full gospel of Christ, and by tailoring its teachings to earth-bound needs and temporal circumstances. Go to an African-dominated church that is located in an area where people have immigration issues and you find that most messages will revolve around immigration. Go to a church filled with the elderly and listen mostly to messages on healing and the hope of eternal life after death. Go to a church full of young people, and the sermons will focus on holiness or all the current social issues affecting the youth. Although such messages are necessary, does such a constantly soft diet really build up muscle to equip the saints for the war they have to fight in faith? Focusing on the problem is certainly not the best way to find a solution.

Word-centred teaching

The Word of God specifies the only way to obtain faith: *"...faith comes from hearing the message, and the message is heard through the word about Christ" (Romans 10:17).* The gospel of 'handouts in the name of compassion' is helping nobody. On the contrary, it is rendering today's church quite powerless compared to the militant early church. Unless the local church pauses to reflect on the biblical reasons explaining why instant miracles have become so scarce in our days, we would continue driving people in fuel-less vehicles.

The Bible shows us exactly what the church should do for empowerment:

> *While Peter was still speaking these words, the Holy Spirit came on all who heard the message. The circumcised believers who had come with Peter were astonished that the gift of the Holy Spirit had been poured out even on Gentiles. For they heard them speaking in tongues and praising God (Acts 10:44).*

Yes, *"the Holy Spirit came on all who heard the message."* When He hears some messages being preached today, He does not manifest because He does not come to be a spectator! It is worth checking what that message was all about and comparing it with the message Peter delivered that momentous Pentecost morning:

> *Then Peter began to speak: "I now realize how true it is that God does not show favouritism but accepts from every nation the one who fears him and does*

what is right. You know the message God sent to the people of Israel, announcing the good news of peace through Jesus Christ, who is Lord of all. You know what has happened throughout the province of Judea, beginning in Galilee after the baptism that John preached—how God anointed Jesus of Nazareth with the Holy Spirit and power, and how he went around doing good and healing all who were under the power of the devil because God was with him.

We are witnesses of everything he did in the country of the Jews and in Jerusalem. They killed him by hanging him on a cross, but God raised him from the dead on the third day and caused him to be seen. He was not seen by all the people, but by witnesses whom God had already chosen—by us who ate and drank with him after he rose from the dead. He commanded us to preach to the people and to testify that he is the one whom God appointed as judge of the living and the dead. All the prophets testify about him that everyone who believes in him receives forgiveness of sins through his name" (Acts 10:34-43).

The message was all about Jesus, the power of the resurrection, the inheritance of all the saints! It was about the awesomeness of judgement day and the need to believe and repent in Jesus' name. However, instead of making Jesus Christ, His death and resurrection as the centrepiece of our preaching, we have delivered shallow messages that do not release faith and, frankly, put people to sleep. The truth has been hidden behind unnecessary and prolonged praise and worship that sometimes leaves very little time for the Word of God to be preached: more and more assemblies have allocated two-thirds of the time of service to singing praises and worship to the Lord. There is nothing wrong with that. On the contrary, the Bible not only shows us how important the moments of praise and worship are, but it also tells us that God resides in the praises of His people (see Psalm 22:3). The episode of Paul and Silas in prison (Acts 16:16-40) demonstrates the irrefutable power of this act of surrender to the Almighty. However, when the amount of time left for the preaching of the Word of God in a church service is reduced to a couple of minutes or placed in between church announcements, there is cause for alarm. The Holy Spirit works with and through the Word of God. The verses below show us how both are connected:

The Spirit and the Word call:

> *The Spirit and the bride say, "Come!" And let the one who hears say, "Come!" Let the one who is thirsty come; and let the one who wishes take the free gift of the water of life. (Revelation 22:17).*

> *He called you to this through our gospel, that you might share in the glory of our Lord Jesus Christ (2 Thessalonians 2:14).*

The Spirit and the Word convince:

> *"When he comes, he will prove the world to be in the wrong about sin and righteousness and judgment" (John 16:8).*

> *When the people heard this, they were cut to the heart and said to Peter and the other apostles, 'Brothers, what shall we do?' (Acts 2:37).*

The Spirit and the Word give life:

"The Spirit gives life; the flesh counts for nothing. The words I have spoken to you – they are full of the Spirit and life" (John 6:63).

This is my comfort in my affliction, that Your word has revived me and given me life (Psalms 119:50).

We are born again through the Spirit and the Word:

Jesus answered, "Very truly I tell you, no one can enter the kingdom of God unless they are born of water and the Spirit" (John 3:5).

For you have been born again, not of perishable seed, but of imperishable, through the living and enduring word of God (1 Peter 1:23).

We are washed, sanctified, justified and saved through the Spirit and the Word:

But you were washed, you were sanctified, you were justified in the name of the Lord Jesus Christ and by the Spirit of our God (1 Corinthians 6:11).

...to make her holy, cleansing her by the washing with water through the word (Ephesians 5:26).

"Sanctify them by the truth; your word is truth" (John 17:17).

Therefore, get rid of all moral filth and the evil that is so prevalent and humbly accept the word planted in you, which can save you (James 1:21).

The Spirit and the Word empower us and set us free:

Now I commit you to God and to the word of his grace, which can build you up and give you an inheritance among all those who are sanctified (Acts 20:32).

Jesus said, "If you hold to my teaching, you are really my disciples. Then you will know the truth, and the truth will set you free" (John 8:31-32).

...because through Christ Jesus the law of the Spirit who gives life has set you free from the law of sin and death (Romans 8:2).

Definitely, the Church cannot be content to relegate the Word of God to the background by favouring praise and worship that may make people feel good as music soothes the soul. It is inconceivable that our assemblies' praise and worship times do not produce earthquakes and breakthroughs in the spiritual realm. This perhaps explains the need for churches to lengthen the worship session to stimulate a sort of anointing flow as if we could coax the Holy Spirit to manifest. Maybe the time has come to wonder how many believers actually understand the intended purpose of corporate praise and worship. To answer this question, this is what the Bible says in Psalm 22:22-23: *"I will declare your name to my people; in the assembly I will praise you. You who fear the Lord, praise him!"* This verse makes a crucial point: that the fear of God must be the foundation of our praise to God. We are challenged here: *"You who fear the Lord, praise him!"* Similarly, Psalm 111 demonstrates that it is equally essential for an assembly of worshippers to praise God with their whole hearts: *"Praise the Lord. I will extol the Lord with all my heart in the council of the upright and in the assembly"* (Psalm 111:1).

The lack of understanding of this underlying concept distorts church-goers' praise and worship offerings: saying or lip-singing glory to God without reverence is vain. How many people do not value the time of praise and worship (because they think it makes church service longer) and choose to go to church later than the time the service is supposed to start, or in the middle of the service? What would happen if we chose to arrive at work late every time? The fear of being sacked is enough to motivate every reasonable person to go to work on time, even during adverse weather or sometimes when feeling unwell. Now, when it comes to going to the house of God, the same reasonable person sometimes becomes insensible enough to believe that there are no consequences for their lack of respect to God. Fearing God is respecting and revering Him! That includes our praise and worship. And not only that:

> *Fear the Lord, you his holy people, for those who fear him lack nothing (Psalm 34:9).*

> *He provides food for those who fear him; he remembers his covenant forever (Psalm 111:5).*

Indeed, the reason we should also fear the Lord is that it opens doors to our divine provision. This leads to the conclusion that, prolonging the time of praise and worship to mask our lack of reverence to God has become tremendously detrimental to many local churches: a pastor who arrives late to the service but expects and demands to be honoured by the congregation… that is an abomination to God who gave His only begotten Son for us to be redeemed. Why? Because, the fact that a pastor comes late signals to the congregation that it does not matter if they, too, are late to worship the Lord. How can such a pastor then correct a church member who can also blame them for the same issue?

So, as seen through the verses above, shortening the Word of God as well as not revering God through our attitude, our language, our dress during our corporate worship does not encourage the release of the Spirit that gives life. Thus, when the Holy Spirit's activity is limited at our meetings, we try to compensate by mimicking Him with hype and speaking on His behalf through our intuition and human understanding rather than revelation.

Compare the genuine article with the counterfeit. Clairvoyants, who do not have the Holy Spirit, can deceive people by telling them accurate facts about their lives! I remember when I was seventeen years old, a young lady reading the palms of my hands predicted I was going to travel a lot in my life. That has indeed happened. But was it a divine message? Certainly not! She predicted so many other things I have never seen such as giving birth to many children. And, serving God over the last seven years, I have realised that, when God speaks, He is precise. God cannot tell you something and leave your mind confused or wandering.

Many believers in the local church have been prayed for or have received prophecies year in year out, but no change has occurred in their lives. This is not the Church of Christ. The Church Christ established has the light and the power to bring people out of darkness no matter how deep or wide. But that Church needs to be focused on Jesus and the true gospel. Only that, not people's individual problems or circumstances, stirs up the faith that pleases God and produces genuine change. Otherwise, the Church is nurturing needy believers instead of raising mature Christians who can grow to become disciples and reach the world one day.

Let's look back at the way Peter witnessed to Cornelius and his household in Acts 10 above. Peter did not start with endless praise and worship to warm their spirits or wake them up. He did not have to perform a long one-man show prayer. He did not start a sermon about who they were or their individual needs; he did not turn the gathering into a prophetic meeting to show that God speaks to him or that he is a true servant of God. He certainly knew about the background of Cornelius and his family because he had invited the three men that had been sent by Cornelius to stay with him (see Acts 10:23). So, we can imagine that he was fully briefed.

Fair enough, Peter was ministering to a small group of people here. Even so, we can see how the Holy Spirit moved freely with no need to warm up their hearts because they must have been prepared for this meeting and expectant. This should remind us that our worship services cannot follow a strict routine or a pattern, just to prepare people to enter the presence of the Lord. Instead, the Church should teach people what God expects of them while in the assembly, how to enter His presence with genuine praises and thanksgiving and to worship Him in Spirit and in truth.

It is also true that the early church, which was almost exclusively composed of Jewish people, replicated the worship practices from the Temple. But what made them peculiar, at that time, was their Christ-centred, Scripture-based, God-fearing worship, which encouraged the believers to learn to be devoted to Jesus. When we are devoted to someone or to a cause, we won't need to be warmed up to welcome that person or that cause. The Bible says: *"I rejoiced with those who said to me, 'Let us go to the house of the Lord'"* *(Psalm 122:1)*. This means that if churches focus on anything else, without applying the teachings, principles and methods of worshipping God learned from Jesus and developed by the early Christians, our way of serving cannot be effective.

Now, let's return to Acts 10 where the Bible tells us that as soon as Peter found himself before the people he was to minister to, he only focused on the message of Christ: what Christ had done for humanity, which produced enough faith in them for the Spirit of God to manifest! This was the power of the early Church. And this power was displayed throughout the ministries of the apostles by instant healings, deliverances, diverse miracles and, above all, conversions by the thousand. This was effective because the church's focus was on exercising the authority and power they were given through the name of Jesus.

Today's church still has the same power and authority. Yet, the lack of Christ-centred preaching in local churches has undermined its efficacy. The preacher's persuasive eloquence or theological sophistication takes precedence over the simple unvarnished preaching of Christ. Let's not forget that God chose one way by which His people would obtain faith: sharing the true gospel of Jesus, which paves the way for faith! So, what should a church of Christ need but Christ Himself?

Christ-centred devotion

We also learn from the books of Acts that believers used to gather together in different houses every day and bring with them all the food they had so they could share with others. The early church did not compel people to give tithes, offerings or alms. People just knew and were willing to give because they understood the church was not man's business but Christ's. Above all, they had the faith that encourages obedience, willingness and action:

They devoted themselves to the apostles' teaching and
to fellowship, to the breaking of bread and to prayer
(Acts 2:42).

"They devoted themselves... to the teaching, fellowship, breaking of bread and prayer." Alleluia! The early Christians were not going to church because of devotion to any human figure but to the purposes of Christ.

"If you devote yourself, your time, or your energy to something, you spend all or most of your time or energy on it," says the Collins English Dictionary. This description matches the biblical definition of what devotion must look like. People devoted to God are necessarily transformed by the renewing of their minds, enough for them to honour Him, pray to Him, and practise love, compassion and forgiveness towards others. People have mistaken concepts about devotion and prayer: We can be devoted to God even without being prayerful. But our prayers need our devotion because being devoted is an attitude expressed through our demonstration of love and loyalty to God. To clarify this, it is important to recall that ever since we became born again, the life of Christ has been in us, and one way to nourish that life is through prayer. That is the reason why Jesus warns us that when we pray only to ask God for earthly things, we are doing exactly like the pagans: *"Therefore do not worry, saying, 'What shall we eat?' or 'What shall we drink?' or 'What shall we wear?' For the pagans strive after all these things, and your Heavenly Father knows that you need them" (Matthew*

6:31-32). Thus, the purpose of prayer is to get to know God, as we draw near Him, communicating with Him and the things of Heaven. Knowing that God aims to change us from the inside out, we should then understand that our prayers are not meant to change things externally but to change our inner nature, so that, in turn, we may change things through the power of God working in and through us.

Therefore, devotion is to display love and dedication to God. One good way of describing it, though we do not support it as no biblical evidence advocates it, is the way the Roman Catholics are devoted to Mary. Not only do they pray to her, but they also honour her with pilgrimages, dedicated places to communicate with her, and so on. But, when we look at the Word of God, we can see that devotion goes beyond God Himself as even the things we offer to God are meant to be devoted to Him: *"But nothing that a person owns and devotes to the LORD--whether a human being or an animal or family land--may be sold or redeemed; everything so devoted is most holy to the Lord" (Leviticus 27:28).* So, we should understand that everything we set aside for God and the Kingdom of God (money, time, strength, possessions, etc.) is part of our devotion. Now, devoting something to God means it cannot be used for personal interest.

Devotion is very important to God and we should remember that, in this time, when we tend to desacralize the things of God, there can be consequences for our negligence:

> *But the Israelites were unfaithful in regard to the devoted things; Achan son of Karmi, the son of Zimri, the son of Zerah, of the tribe of Judah, took some of them. So, the Lord's anger burned against Israel (Joshua 7:1).*

Following this, Israel lost the battle against Ai, and God told Joshua why it happened:

> *"Israel has sinned; they have violated my covenant, which I commanded them to keep. They have taken some of the devoted things; they have stolen, they have lied, they have put them with their own possessions. That is why the Israelites cannot stand against their enemies" (Joshua 7:10-12).*

Similarly, after Ananias and Sapphira claimed they had devoted all of the money received from the sale of their property to God having hidden part of it for their personal use, they died (Acts 5:1-11). Why? Their lying revealed a private agenda to withhold money that had ostensibly been set apart to the Lord. True devotion stems from our willingness to faithfully serve the Lord. Thus, we should always examine ourselves and ensure that we have genuinely devoted ourselves to God and *"to one another in love" (Romans 12:10)* and that everything we have given the Lord serves Him and not our own interests. Jesus said: *"No one can serve two masters. Either you will hate the one and love the other, or you will be devoted to the one and despise the other. You cannot serve both God and money" (Matthew 6:24).*

Christ-centred fellowship

Because the early Christians *"devoted themselves to the apostles' teaching and to fellowship, to the breaking of bread and to prayer" (Acts 2:42)*, it inevitably produced spiritual fruit. God used the apostles to perform signs and wonders and the believers practised generosity with one another as well as close fellowship.

> *Everyone was filled with awe at the many wonders and signs performed by the apostles. All the believers were together and had everything in common. They sold property and possessions to give to anyone who had need. Every day they continued to meet together in the temple courts. They broke bread in their homes and ate together with glad and sincere hearts, praising God and enjoying the favor of all the people. And the Lord added to their number daily those who were being saved (Acts 2:43-47).*

The above passage indicates that the lives of the servants of God can be enhanced when they are in fellowship with a devoted and close-knit congregation. For that purpose too, deacons were appointed to take care of the people's ordinary needs:

> *Therefore, brothers, select from among you seven men confirmed to be full of the Spirit and wisdom. We will appoint this responsibility to them and devote ourselves to prayer and to the ministry of the word (Acts 6:3).*

Obviously, the world has evolved since those open-hearted early days, and the church has inevitably suffered from the passage of time. Today, most churches are filled with people who are unwilling to fellowship with other believers. They have not understood that the church of Christ is about togetherness and unity, where two or three people gather in His name to praise and worship Him.

Controlling leaders

The self-centred interests of many of today's church leaders have made more and more people reluctant to devote themselves fully to Kingdom work. While the servants of God of the past stood out in their service to God, many local churches are today plagued by the leadership of uncrucified men or women who behave as if they established the Church, viewing the people of God as their own possessions.

Nowhere does the Bible encourage us to put pressure on the people of God for church needs, church growth or church finances, and so on. The early Christians had a proclivity for giving that we don't find in the believers of today. Shouldn't we wonder why there is such a disparity between the early church and the twenty-first-century church that, paradoxically, has much greater means than their predecessors? Without a doubt, a return to the fundamentals is vital for the Church to continuously experience the transforming power intended by God.

In the meantime, too many human contrivances are undermining the principles of God such as setting the amount of offerings believers should give, selling anointed or healing water or oils with bottles carrying the image of the pastor, etc. This leaves many believers puzzled, hungry for the truth, searching and unsatisfied without being able to say what they truly lack. I once had a conversation with a teenage girl whom I was teaching as she had refused to allow me to touch one of her pens because it was 'anointed' My efforts were useless when I tried to explain to her that she was anointed, but her pen had no power. When she added that in their church, the pastor was anointing lipsticks that women could buy as well as a long list of other useful items, I just resolved to remain silent. How then can we expect such people to be devoted to Christ or to give to the church in faith for His work? Instead, they would rather exchange their devotion to God for 'anointed' things and for 'anointed' servants of God; and their gift to God would instead be traded for blessings prophesied by the servants of God.

Numbers over transformed lives

All this leads us to affirm that, when a church or a ministry is faith-based rather than dependent on the headcount of church members, Christ will take His rightful place in their midst and the Holy Spirit will move. As a matter of fact, the number of people in a church does not count because what is essential is the quality displayed by the transformation of character, faith in action and the practice of the Word of God. Yet, the urge to crowd the church with seat-fillers often gives rise to disinterest in the Word itself. Jesus never told His disciples to fill the church. He commissioned them to make disciples!

The church is a family in Christ, born out of the will of the Father who wants to unite His children under one name: Jesus Christ. Thus, the Church is supposed to model love and unity to both Christians and non-Christians alike. Now, just like in any family, hardship can hit, affecting different areas in the church including the brethren or the pastoral teams, human resources, finances, equipment, and so on. In such times, the church should lean on the Head, just like any family would expect the head of the family to bring about solutions. Yet, despite knowing that God provides faithfully and that He may do it instantly or gradually for His work in the Body of Christ to advance, too much pressure is put on the church members concerning those needs so much so that some become overwhelmed and discouraged enough to leave the church. That's the main problem with today's church!

Globally, too, church needs have taken precedence over the message of hope, patience and faith in the Mighty One so freely displayed throughout Jesus' ministry on earth. It was adopted by the first disciples and apostles, who, contrary to what has become a general trend, did not foist the expenses of their ministries on to people, hoping that they would support them. For example, though in full-time ministry, Apostle Paul continued to work as a tentmaker to support himself and his ministry of witnessing Christ:

> *After this, Paul left Athens and went to Corinth. There he met a Jew named Aquila, a native of Pontus, who had recently come from Italy with his wife Priscilla, because Claudius had ordered all Jews to leave Rome. Paul went to see them, and because he was a tentmaker as they were, he stayed and worked with them (Acts 18:1-3).*

In other words, Apostle Paul considered that using the money he earned for the ministry was part of his service to God. He would then work to be able to use his earnings not to burden people:

> *And for the sake of your souls, I will most gladly spend my money and myself. If I love you more, will you love me less? Be that as it may, I was not a burden to you (2 Corinthians 12:16).*

Undeniably, Apostle Paul is showing those who claim to serve Jesus that he himself toiled to help those in need and he showed himself generous in giving, as Jesus Himself taught. This reminds us of what Luke says when he declares that the Spirit of God urges us to give and use all the resources at our disposal for the sake of our communities as a witness to the gospel:

> *Give, and it will be given to you. A good measure, pressed down, shaken together and running over, will be poured into your lap. For with the measure you use, it will be measured to you (Luke 6:38).*

Everything is possible with God since He is not limited in time, space and certainly not in material provision and finances. So, when did money become the cornerstone of the church instead of Christ? When has the number of attendees become the cornerstone of the church instead of Christ? When have music instruments become the cornerstone of the church instead of Christ? Though the answer may depend on where a local church is located geographically, as the practices concerning church provisions depend on that, sometimes, the damage caused to individuals is so deeply rooted that many church-goers are saved but all the same feel 'lost'. They are unable to settle in their faith and become spiritually paralysed, as focusing on a church's financial or numerical increase instead of feeding the believers to allow them to grow in the knowledge of Christ, somehow affects the entire body of Christ.

This book is not a recipe for success or a self-improvement manual. It is an urgent call to the church and to every individual who confesses Christ as Lord and Saviour to return to the fundamentals and foundations of the early Church. Abide in Christ and promote the Kingdom of God instead of being more concerned with temporal mundane matters.

Chapter II
The Pre-eminence of the Holy Spirit

The believers in the Bible understood very well that the church is the body of Christ, *"the fullness of him who fills everything in every way" (Ephesians 1:23).* They understood that the head is Jesus and the Holy Spirit takes control over all our worship.

By contrast, idolatry has moved and settled in so strongly in today's Pentecostal charismatic church that a substitute spirit has taken over certain churches and leading them astray. It appears that the Holy Spirit is sitting in the back row of many denominations, waiting to be given the space to help, comfort or empower people according to the Scriptures. Thus, His role has been reduced to that of a simple messenger who receives commands to jump to attention when need be: 'Holy Ghost, fire!', 'Holy Spirit, heal!', 'Holy Spirit, take control!' In practice, though, the servants of God tend to do everything because they are so 'anointed'. We need to remind the Church that the Holy Spirit is part of the Godhead. He is sent to everyone who would accept Jesus Christ as Lord and Saviour and be baptised in Him.

Before the day of the Pentecost, even Jesus needed the Spirit's contribution in many instances to carry out the will and plans of God. For example, the Holy Spirit descended on Jesus after His baptism (Matthew 3:16); the Holy Spirit led Jesus to the wilderness to be tempted (Matthew 4:1); the Spirit was poured on Jesus Christ without measure (John 3:34). Regrettably, today's church has marginalised the Holy Spirit by reducing His roles to the gifts He gives or the miracles He performs.

Needless to say, the void caused in the Church is huge as no spiritual war can be won without the help and guidance of the Spirit of God. Why? Because when Jesus was about to leave the earth, He said to His disciples: *"I am going to the Father... I will ask Him to send you **another** comforter" (John 14:16, emphasis added)*. When Jesus was physically on earth, He was there to help and comfort us. He then made sure the Holy Spirit would be sent in His place to be our helper and comforter in the many spiritual battles we face.

A straightforward definition of the word 'spiritual' is related to the Spirit (the Holy Spirit), the human spirit (which should not be mistaken for the human soul) or demonic entities. Now, the Bible says, *"our struggle is not against flesh and blood, but against the rulers, against the authorities, against the powers of this dark world and against the spiritual forces of evil in the heavenly realms" (Ephesians 6:12)*. So, if the Spirit of God is absent within a church, only two other invisible spirits remain: ours and demons. If we constrain the work of the Holy Spirit, we set ourselves up as a carnal church or, worse still, we open ourselves to the infiltration of demons. Many see the present church as lukewarm and apathetic, not much different from the church in Laodicea:

> *I counsel you to buy from me gold refined in the fire, so you can become rich; and white clothes to wear, so you*

> *can cover your shameful nakedness; and salve to put on
> your eyes, so you can see. Those whom I love I rebuke and
> discipline. So be earnest and repent. Here I am! I stand at
> the door and knock. If anyone hears my voice and opens
> the door, I will come in and eat with that person, and they
> with me (Revelation 3:18-20).*

The Laodicean church was materially wealthy because of their flourishing trade in purple dye. But they were blinded to their spiritual poverty. In our Godless fast-evolving society, the church can no longer close its eyes to our own poverty, blindness and lack of power. This underlines the urgent need to operate in all its power through the Holy Spirit.

Call for unity

Jesus will only be manifested in the Church through the indwelling of the Holy Spirit in the believers. The invitation for the Church to return to Him has never been more urgent than now, especially in times of blatant perversions and unprecedented atrocities around the world. As the Church allows the Holy Spirit to rekindle His fire in us, the power of God will manifest to bring glory to the Lord Almighty. For this to happen, unity is imperative because one and the same Spirit of God is operating in every believer of Christ:

> *And if the Spirit of him who raised Jesus from the dead is
> living in you, he who raised Christ from the dead will also
> give life to your mortal bodies because of his Spirit who
> lives in you (Romans 8:11).*

This unity is needed also for God to fulfil His plans on earth through the Church that is equipped for this purpose:

> *To one there is given through the Spirit a message of wisdom, to another a message of knowledge by means of the same Spirit, to another faith by the same Spirit, to another gifts of healing by that one Spirit, to another miraculous powers, to another prophecy, to another distinguishing between spirits, to another speaking in different kinds of tongues, and to still another the interpretation of tongues. All these are the work of one and the same Spirit, and he distributes them to each one, just as he determines. Just as a body, though one, has many parts, but all its many parts form one body, so it is with Christ (1 Corinthians 12:8-12).*

The church's unity is in Christ, the Head of the body. And this unity is required to give the Holy Spirit the rightful place that is His in the Church as seen in Acts 10:44. Indeed, while Peter was preaching the gospel of Jesus Christ, the Holy Spirit fell on those who were listening to the Word. Surely, they must have been listening actively! In this passage we are told that the Holy Spirit took control and did what He had to do, leaving amazed the believers accompanying Peter, who were used to a certain protocol for the baptism of the Holy Spirit:

> *The circumcised believers who had come with Peter were astonished that the gift of the Holy Spirit had been poured out even on Gentiles. For they heard them speaking in tongues and praising God (Acts 10:45-46).*

This is what should happen in our assemblies all the time. How often do we witness these kinds of manifestation in our different church gatherings nowadays? In fact, the Holy Spirit is not given the opportunity to do His part anymore, not only because many believers go to church unprepared for His visitation, but also, because the servants of God tend to ignore Him. Every believer understands that the Holy Spirit dwells in us, but many lack the knowledge of who He is and what His role is. Thus, it is common to hear confessing believers of Christ insist that His indwelling presence allows them to neglect the assembly, while the Bible clearly says:

> *And let us consider how we may spur one another on toward love and good deeds, not giving up meeting together, as some are in the habit of doing, but encouraging one another—and all the more as you see the Day approaching (Hebrews 10:24-25).*

Allow the Holy Spirit to act in full power

Calling on the Holy Spirit is not enough if we are calling upon Him in name only! The book of Acts recounts great miracles and God's intervention in human plans when the Holy Spirit was expected to come in power. For instance, we read about the great outpouring of the Holy Spirit on the day of Pentecost with people speaking in unknown tongues (Acts 2:2-6), deliverances (Acts 16:16), healings (Acts 3:1-10; Acts 9:32-35; Acts 28:8), people raised from the dead (Acts 9:36-4; Acts 20:7-12), and many more.

What is incredible is that the book of Acts is preached over and over in churches and people will tell you about some of those outstanding miracles. Nevertheless, very little attention is devoted to cultivating the presence of the Holy Spirit. He has been the main actor of the church since the early days. He is the power within the Church, and without Him, the Church is hopeless and ineffective. The Church is the place to demonstrate the presence of the Holy Spirit, for it is He who inspires the servants of God for effective ministry:

> *"...for it will not be you speaking, but the Spirit of your Father speaking through you" (Matthew 10:20).*

> *"When you are brought before synagogues, rulers and authorities, do not worry about how you will defend yourselves or what you will say, for the Holy Spirit will teach you at that time what you should say" (Luke 12:11-12).*

Through the teachings of Apostle Paul, we can see that the Holy Spirit was very active within the church community, which implies the necessity for unity (coming together as one). In other words, despite the diversity of the people, the Holy Spirit was seen as the unifying figure whose role was to guide the Church towards one body in Christ:

> *For we were all baptized by one Spirit so as to form one body – whether Jews or Gentiles, slave or free-- and we were all given the one Spirit to drink (1 Corinthians 12:13).*

Moreover, the Holy Spirit reminds us of all the things that Jesus had taught:

> *"But the Advocate, the Holy Spirit, whom the Father will send in My name, will teach you all things and will remind you of everything I have told you" (John 14:26).*

And that is not all. The Holy Spirit helps us to lead a life that is disciplined and does not gratify the flesh:

> *So, I say, walk by the Spirit, and you will not gratify the desires of the flesh. For the flesh desires what is contrary to the Spirit, and the Spirit what is contrary to the flesh. They are in conflict with each other, so that you are not to do whatever you want. But if you are led by the Spirit, you are not under the law… But the fruit of the Spirit is love, joy, peace, forbearance, kindness, goodness, faithfulness, gentleness and self-control. Against such things there is no law. Those who belong to Christ Jesus have crucified the flesh with its passions and desires. Since we live by the Spirit, let us keep in step with the Spirit. Let us not become conceited, provoking and envying each other (Galatians 5:16-18, 22-26).*

> *For those who are led by the Spirit of God are the children of God. The Spirit you received does not make you slaves, so that you live in fear again; rather, the Spirit you received brought about your adoption to sonship. And by him we cry, "Abba, Father." The Spirit himself testifies with our spirit that we are God's children. Now if we are children, then we are heirs—heirs of God and co-heirs with Christ, if indeed we share in his sufferings in order that we may also share in his glory (Romans 8:14-17).*

Unfortunately, in today's church the spotlight is now given to church leaders as much as the emphasis is put on charismatic gifts (namely, messages of wisdom, messages of knowledge, increased faith, gifts of healing, the gift of miracles, prophecy, the discernment of spirits, speaking in tongues or interpretation of tongues according to 1 Corinthians 12:8-10) rather than on the Holy Spirit Himself. The Epistles remind Christians of the importance of not gratifying the flesh (Galatians 5:16-18) as well as the necessity of developing spiritual fruit (Galatians 5:22-26), which shows the genuine transformation from the inside out. Should we then be surprised that phenomenal charismatic moves of the Spirit have become scarce in today's church?

Claiming that we have the indwelling presence of the Holy Spirit does not guarantee that God is using us, and certainly not that we have any spiritual gift. A gift is a GIFT… And the Bible says:

> *There are different kinds of gifts, but the same Spirit distributes them. There are different kinds of service, but the same Lord. There are different kinds of working, but in all of them and in everyone it is the same God at work. Now to each one the manifestation of the Spirit is given for the common good. To one there is given through the Spirit a message of wisdom, to another a message of knowledge by means of the same Spirit, to another faith by the same Spirit, to another gifts of healing by that one Spirit, to another miraculous powers, to another prophecy, to another distinguishing between spirits, to another speaking in different kinds of tongues, and to still another the interpretation of tongues. All these are the work of one and the same Spirit, and he distributes them to each one, just as he determines (1 Corinthians 12:4-11).*

The manifestation of the Spirit has been a source of discord among the believers since the beginning. Remember that Apostle Paul had to defend his calling and respond to those in Corinth criticising his ministry by stressing that the weakness they saw in him pointed to the power of God at work in and through him (2

Corinthians 10:1-11). Indeed, the power of God can work through our weaknesses, and most importantly, even without any visible evidence. This needs to be mentioned here as some people believe that the Holy Spirit's manifestation is automatically accompanied by visible supernatural signs, such as falling, crying, shouting, rolling on the floor, etc., so much that they have become sign-runners. If they attend a church service and none of the signs they expect to see happen, they return with the feeling that nothing has happened, or assume the servant of God is not anointed 'enough'.

On one occasion, during a conversation with a pastor who had invited me to preach at his church, I was surprised to hear him speaking about his sign-hungry congregation in these terms: 'If there is no sign during a service (meaning: people falling, prophecies, healings or deliverances), they would leave the meeting unsatisfied.' What a pressure on a preacher of the Word of God! It is true that Jesus advocated signs and wonders (Mark 16:18-20); the disciples displayed them after the resurrection, and the church, in general, should expect manifestations as often as we preach the Word of God. Still, a gift of the Spirit is nothing but a GIFT and does not depend on any servant of God! Every sign or charismatic manifestation stems from the Spirit of God who works through us, and the Church should be taught not to be demanding on servants of God to manifest them, lest we want to encourage fake anointing in our midst.

I remember a church meeting where we prayed for many people. A lady called the following day in tears saying, that when she returned home, she found out God had healed her. She had a visible, physical infirmity but nothing seemed to happen to her during the prayer meeting. Nevertheless, the Holy Spirit had manifested His power by healing Her, despite showing no evident sign during the meeting.

Defining how the Holy Spirit is supposed to operate within an assembly is pure human fabrication as the Lord works in mysterious ways (Isaiah 45:15). No surprise, in fact, since the Holy Spirit has been reduced to a mere messenger. In addition to this, He has been depicted as a faultfinder or a gossiper who exposes people's sins or personal matters publicly, which scares away unbelievers who witness such things. Isn't it the result of immaturity? As we already mentioned, the Holy Spirit works through men and women, called and entrusted by Jesus for ministry as seen on the passage below:

> *So Christ himself gave the apostles, the prophets, the evangelists, the pastors and teachers, to equip his people for works of service, so that the body of Christ may be built up until we all reach unity in the faith and in the knowledge of the Son of God and become mature, attaining to the whole measure of the fullness of Christ (Ephesians 4:11-13).*

So, what causes such immaturity, if not the pressure compelling servants of God to manifest spiritual gifts at all cost, even when unprepared or uninspired? Anyone who is wise and spiritually inspired would not fall into deception when a preacher delivers prophetic messages out of his own flesh. Which of the saints could be equipped when they are embarrassed by an 'inspired' message delivered publicly which puts them down? How many people have left the church (or never returned to a church after being given a 'prophetic message?' Doesn't the Spirit, when giving messages, also provide us with wisdom and discernment? The Bible says:

> *The Spirit of the Lord will rest on him – the Spirit of wisdom and of understanding, the Spirit of counsel and of might, the Spirit of the knowledge and fear of the Lord – and he will delight in the fear of the Lord (Isaiah 11:2).*

All too often, intuition and personal opinion have been used by unscrupulous servants of God pretending to speak on behalf of the Spirit of God, in an attempt to undermine or manipulate the believers. Unfortunately, when such messages fall on the itching ears of vulnerable individuals or spiritually immature believers, a lot of damage can be caused. In 2010, a certain prophetess of God told us (my brother and me) to avoid our mother. My brother tried to stop me from visiting or even eating at our mum's place as he had been doing for some time. I thank God for giving me the discernment quick enough, to see what was wrong in this lady. Once, she had asked me to give her money to pray for me after I told her I had had a bad dream. I started avoiding her calls claiming that Jesus Christ had died for me and that I should not pay anyone to be prayed for. How many people fall into such false anointing for material gain that is meant to exploit people's vulnerabilities?

As children of God, we need to be aware that the trauma of a false anointing can lead us to extreme and satanic behaviours while believing our actions are approved by the Lord. How many people, like my brother, have been deceived by a false prophecy or a false anointing? Nowhere in the Bible do we see Jesus instigate suspicion or hatred for people. On the contrary, the Bible tells us that God is love. So, any message from God that does not promote love cannot come from God:

> *It does not dishonor others, it is not self-seeking, it is not easily angered, it keeps no record of wrongs. Love does not delight in evil but rejoices with the truth. It always protects, always trusts, always hopes, always perseveres. Love never fails. But where there are prophecies, they will cease; where there are tongues, they will be stilled; where there is knowledge, it will pass away. For we know in part and we prophesy in part, but when completeness comes, what is in part disappears. When I was a child, I talked like a child, I thought like a child, I reasoned like a child. When I became a man, I put the ways of childhood behind me. For now, we see only a reflection as in a mirror; then we shall see face to face. Now I know in part; then I shall know fully, even as I am fully known. And now these three remain: faith, hope and love. But the greatest of these is love (1 Corinthians 13:5-13).*

Love is what you evaluate prophecies with! God Himself, spoke to the children of Israel through His prophets to lead them back to Him, and certainly not away from Him, whenever they disappointed or disobeyed Him. The story of Jonah is eloquent in itself. God sent

Jonah to Nineveh because He had already decided to let His judgment fall on the people of Nineveh. But owing to His love for them, He relented because He had compassion on them as see in Jonah 4:11:

<blockquote>"And should I not have concern for the great city of Nineveh, in which there are more than a hundred and twenty thousand people who cannot tell their right hand from their left – and also many animals?"</blockquote>

In other words, God is telling us to stop judging people, especially those who lack spiritual knowledge and discernment. Instead, we should allow the Spirit of God to convict people while doing what the Bible says: displaying love not suspicion, showing understanding and compassion instead of spreading subjective conclusions about people. Nobody on earth, whether Christian or not, baptised or not, has the legal right to condemn someone to hell because the salvation offered by Jesus is such a mystery that the thief on the Cross alongside Jesus took the opportunity to accept Jesus before his last breath, and went to heaven. Surely, people who knew him would remember him as nothing but a thief, but Jesus opened the door to Paradise to that 'thief' because he repented (Luke 23:39-43).

This leads us to conclude that if the Church (leaders and members) persist in not allowing the Holy Spirit the liberty to move as He wishes in today's Church, Christianity, that already has bad connotations, will end up becoming irrelevant. This will undeniably pave the way to growing practices of idolatry or witchcraft before the very eyes of blinded believers who are hungry for one thing: miracles! The church has never been established to promote miracles in and of themselves but to lead people to Jesus.

Jesus' church has a clear commission and the Holy Spirit plays a major role in its fulfilment: *"Go and make disciples of all nations, baptizing them in the name of the Father and of the Son and of the Holy Spirit, and teaching them to obey everything I have commanded you" (Matthew 28:19-20)*. Instead of taking time to teach people to obey the Word and to allow the Holy Spirit to do His part in them, many ministers perform 'miracles' in churches as means of attracting and retaining people. This has created more miracle-runners who follow 'anointed prophets' from one church to another and find it hard to become stable to grow spiritually.

Yet, the message of the Cross is still powerful, enough to convince someone to follow Jesus wholeheartedly and consistently. This is especially true of our society where people are more and more sceptical and easily disheartened. Indeed, the testimony of Evangelist Nicky Cruz is inspiring as it shows us that the two things that touched him when he was evangelised by David Wilkerson back in 1958, were, first, the non-judgemental approach of the preacher who, despite knowing he was a gang-leader and thief, asked him to collect the offerings of the first church service he ever attended; secondly, what 'finished him' in his words was hearing the preaching of the message of the Cross.

In contrast, putting emphasis on miracles while curtailing the message of the Resurrected Christ with the hope Jesus offers to those who follow Him today can become a huge setback to a believer's growth. It may also give the believer a partial understanding of the Holy Spirit, His role and the significance of His indwelling presence. Consequently, a believer who lacks sound or deep-rooted biblical teaching may experience a fruitless Christian life that moves in a cycle of doubts, unanswered questions, and worse still, confusion and deception that could lead them to search for Christ everywhere except in the Word of God!

Chapter III
The Church: One Message, Many Practices

Diversity of practices

Globally, Christianity has gone through many challenges over the years. And, certainly, in recent years, the pluralistic landscape of denominations inevitably generates different church approaches that are sometimes detrimental both to Christians and the general perception of what the Church is. Thus, despite sharing the same message, a wide variety of forms are applied when it comes to service and ministries. This reminds us of the early days of Christianity when factions had already started within the Church between uncompromising supporters of circumcision and the church leaders.

At that time, some Jews who were newly converted to the teaching of Christ advocated preaching salvation by works. One main leader, Apostle Peter, was among them! In fact, they had not yet understood the message of the Cross. So, they wanted to keep the legalistic requirements of which circumcision was the touchstone as an imposed practice for newly converted Christians. The debate between law and grace was thus brought to its climax when those detractors went to Galatia to try and undermine the preaching of Apostle Paul:

> *Certain people came down from Judea to Antioch and were teaching the believers: "Unless you are*

circumcised, according to the custom taught by Moses, you cannot be saved." This brought Paul and Barnabas into sharp dispute and debate with them. So, Paul and Barnabas were appointed, along with some other believers, to go up to Jerusalem to see the apostles and elders about this question (Acts 15:1-2).

Indeed, after spending more than fourteen years away from Jerusalem, Apostle Paul had been preaching the message of grace to advance the gospel of Christ among the heathens. Now, he needed to return to Jerusalem to meet the most influential apostles of the time in an attempt to discuss the doctrinal conflicts opposing them:

Then after fourteen years, I went up again to Jerusalem, this time with Barnabas. I took Titus along also. I went in response to a revelation and, meeting privately with those esteemed as leaders, I presented to them the gospel that I preach among the Gentiles. I wanted to be sure I was not running and had not been running my race in vain (Galatians 2:1-2).

Here, Apostle Paul says that it was because of revelation that he was going up to Jerusalem. But note that he carefully travelled along with Titus, a Greek convert, who was not circumcised (Galatians 2:3) because he was determined to share his inspired understanding of the teaching he had been spreading among the Gentiles. The fact that he did not mention the names of *"those esteemed as leaders"* should make us understand that the gospel is a matter of personal conviction, not a topic for people's debate because it is the message that is conveyed to the people of God that is important, not the messengers.

This brings us to the point that today's church has suffered the same kind of factionalism that is displayed in the early church. Trends, currents and many doctrinal issues have been put forward in some areas that supersede the message of grace. I remember, once, being invited to a meeting with a man who wanted me to debate about the race of Jesus. He told me I was not teaching the right gospel if I was not teaching about the 'Black Jesus'. I had to walk away from this meeting because it was taking none of us anywhere. As, for this individual, the revelation of grace had not come to his table.

What was happening in Galatia that Apostle Paul went to put right in Jerusalem to avoid confusing believers? It was the poisonous atmosphere stirred up by some leaders who wanted to impose circumcision on Gentile converts. The same atmosphere of discord prevails in certain churches because of factions that want to push their own agendas; this is detrimental to the well-being of the Church in general.

So often, churchgoers tend to hop from church to church over time because of the abundance of choices given to the believers in terms of doctrines, beliefs and even reputation. Looking back, the early believers did not have all these choices, so their main motivation for belonging to a church was being together among fellow worshippers of the Lord Jesus.

That is why, from time to time, it is vital for every believer to self-examine in the light of the Word and settle the reason they are in the church they attend. There are multitudes of churches, and, unfortunately, *"some false believers had infiltrated our ranks to spy on the freedom we have in Christ Jesus and to make us slaves" (Galatians 2:4).* If a church is not faithfully transmitting the gospel message and the obedience of faith, then that church must be focusing on things that do not necessarily help the believers grow to become disciples. Therefore, their spiritual growth will be slowed down or absolutely hampered.

Factionalism and competition

Apostle Paul, in defending his ministry, also proved that God does not encourage favouritism. He himself was not in competition with anyone. He accepted God's mandate to serve Jesus: while Apostle Peter was called to evangelise the circumcised, he was called to reach out to the uncircumcised:

> *As for those who were held in high esteem—whatever they were makes no difference to me; God does not show favoritism—they added nothing to my message. On the contrary, they recognized that I had been entrusted with the task of preaching the gospel to the uncircumcised, just as Peter had been to the circumcised. For God, who was at work in Peter as an apostle to the circumcised, was also at work in me*

as an apostle to the Gentiles. James, Cephas and John, those esteemed as pillars, gave me and Barnabas the right hand of fellowship when they recognized the grace given to me. They agreed that we should go to the Gentiles, and they to the circumcised (Galatians 2:6-9).

But when Peter came to Antioch, I had to oppose him to his face, for what he did was very wrong. When he first arrived, he ate with the Gentile believers, who were not circumcised. But afterward, when some friends of James came, Peter wouldn't eat with the Gentiles anymore. He was afraid of criticism from these people who insisted on the necessity of circumcision. As a result, other Jewish believers followed Peter's hypocrisy, and even Barnabas was led astray by their hypocrisy (Galatians 2:11-13).

These passages definitely reveal that rivalry, contests and hypocrisy have always plagued the Church. And thank God for the tenacity and the determination of Apostle Paul, who worked hard to demonstrate to his peers, and to us, through the inspiration of the Spirit (Galatians 2:2), that factionalism and competition have no place in the church. There may be different ministries but one and the same message, one and the same Spirit. For it is the message, not our various opinions or preferences, that should prevail.

Let's just review the scene recounted in Galatians 2:11-13, which shows us how far legalism can lead even a great servant of God like Apostle Peter astray. Because of his background based on the Old Covenant, as the events unfolded after the Resurrection,

Apostle Peter surely did not fully grasp the implications of the New Covenant. So, he found it unlawful for Jewish people to mingle with the Gentiles publicly, while he did it privately, thereby exposing his own hypocrisy. Worse, his action led Barnabas astray because he must also have been confused. The same is happening in our churches today when we dogmatically insist on observing the letter of the Old Covenant rather than the Spirit. In doing so, we risk leading many believers astray.

To unravel these issues of factionalism and competition within our churches, when the situation calls for it, we should be as bold as Apostle Paul. It is the message that counts, not the messenger; the same God works in each of us. If this God shaped Peter who had denied Jesus, He can shape each of us, too.

Also, unity must triumph in the Body of Christ, especially among those who preach the Word. This implies putting aside arguments or disputes that often blow a harmful wind on the true mission of the Church. Some of these practices include competition for positions within the church, privileges granted to certain groups (especially family members) within the church over others, opinionated positions regarding the service of women in the church, women wearing the veil or trousers in the assembly, etc. Nomism, or the rigid observance of the Law, has no more place in the Church as it did in the early Church, for Jesus fulfilled the Law, paving the way for the grace of God to come to us!

Neglect of personal ministry

Many believers are busy attending church meetings, yet they neglect their own personal ministries. Ministering to the needs of individuals is what God expects from each one of His children to fulfil the Great Commission. Because of church denominations and organisations, a great number of believers are not aware that they are called to be ministers of the Lord, too. The Bible tells us that everyone created by God, whether a believer or not, has been endowed by the Father with certain gifts or talents, even before they were born, to use for the benefit of others:

> *We have different gifts, according to the grace given to each of us. If your gift is prophesying, then prophesy in accordance with your faith; if it is serving, then serve; if it is teaching, then teach; if it is to encourage, then give encouragement; if it is giving, then give generously; if it is to lead, do it diligently; if it is to show mercy, do it cheerfully (Romans 12:6-8).*

This is important to mention as many people have not committed to serving in church nowadays because they think that only some are called to carry out the tasks of the 'ministry'. Also, we are choosy about what we want to do in church. Yet our ministry was decided by God before we knew it because it is He who gives us the grace to serve others in different areas. For example, hospitality that some societies have sometimes regarded as a burden is a ministry in itself. The Bible tells us to *"Share with the Lord's people who are in need. Practice hospitality" (Romans 12:13)* and to *"Offer hospitality to one another without grumbling" (1 Peter 4:9)*. Even giving money to church is a ministry: many women around Jesus were there to give their possessions! Apostle Paul also highlights this ministry of giving as exemplified by the tremendous giving of Barnabas: *"Joseph, a Levite from Cyprus, whom the apostles called Barnabas (which means "son of encouragement"), sold a field he owned and brought the money and put it at the apostles' feet" (Acts 4:36-37)*.

Perhaps, a definition of a church ministry will allow every believer to question themselves at this point about their own ministry or area of activity; according to the Wikipedia online dictionary, 'n Christianity, ministry is an activity carried out by Christians to express or spread their faith, the prototype being the Great Commission.' So, I want to tell every believer of Christ that, instead of spending years asking God to reveal their ministry, they should start serving Him. Look at what God has favoured you with and start using it to express and spread your faith in the Lord.

A young man once told me he wanted to become a pastor. I literally laughed because I know that this person hardly goes to church. My answer was radical: 'You want to become a pastor? Start sitting *"at the Lord's feet listening to what he says"'* (see Luke 10:39). He did not understand this. So, I explained that he could not decide what he wanted to become in the house of God. He first needed to learn to sit like Mary did and learn from the Lord. Today, we sit at the feet of Jesus in the Church to learn and be equipped, nowhere else! Pretending that God, who has shown from the garden of Eden how He loves fellowshipping with man, has asked you to withdraw from the community of believers for years and empowered you to serve Him is a deception from the devil!

Now, when we don't take the time to sit at the feet of the Lord, it means we are standing, and we are getting busy or preoccupied with worldly matters. That will inevitably grow anxiety in us as it happened with Martha who started comparing herself to her sister, and even judging her:

> *But Martha was distracted by all the preparations that had to be made. She came to him and asked, "Lord, don't you care that my sister has left me to do the work by myself? Tell her to help me" (Luke 10:40).*

In fact, Martha was not doing anything wrong as she was serving the Lord, in preparing the house for guests and maybe cooking for Him. However, being so preoccupied with her chores even in His presence, she neglected what was more important: being with Him! And the Bible says, *"Martha was distracted by all the preparations."* The danger in trying to serve the Lord without wisdom and discernment is that we may become bitter, hypocritical or grumblers:

> *"Martha, Martha," the Lord answered, "you are worried and upset about many things, but few things are needed—or indeed only one. Mary has chosen*

what is better, and it will not be taken away from her"
(Luke 10:41-42).

That's what Jesus told Martha. What is He telling you today? Are you founding your walk with Him on the things you do more than on your faith in Him? Serving the Lord should never draw us away from our intimacy with Him. Ministry should not hinder our times alone with the Lord. When do you withdraw from the crowd to be refilled? Many times, after ministering to people the whole day in the streets of Jerusalem, Jesus would go away to be alone: *"But Jesus often withdrew to lonely places and prayed"* (Luke *5:16)*. Remember that on earth, Jesus was the Son of Man. These are the moments He would have to withdraw to receive from Heaven the strength and anointing that would work on Him and through Him when ministering. The battle on the Cross was won that night before the Cross when He was praying to God... not on the day He was arrested or crucified.

Allow me to share my testimony about the amazing strength that comes from spending time in the presence of the Lord. Almost three years ago, ten days after losing a loved one and preparing to travel for his funeral in Ghana, I had a Bible study. In the middle of my preaching, I said something like this: 'I feel in my spirit I need to wake up tonight at 3.00 am and pray.' I did not know why I was saying this as this thought had popped up in my spirit just like that. After the Bible study, as we were leaving the building, I repeated the same thing to the pastor who was walking by my side: 'I must go to bed early to wake up at 3.00 am and pray tonight.'

Interestingly enough, that night I woke up to pray before my alarm rang. Since I did not really know why I was being led to pray by the Spirit, I prayed in tongues mostly. The following morning, I had an appointment at the Ghanaian embassy in London to get the visas. I had been waiting to be received for about two hours, when, around 1.00 pm, just when it was my turn to go to the counter, I received a message on my phone that I peeked at on my way to the counter. As I was standing there, I checked the message again to read that one of my brothers had been found dead in his bedroom. So, in the space of ten days, while still helping my children to deal with the loss of their dad in Ghana, I now had to deal with the loss of my brother in Cameroon.

Instead of bursting into tears or feeling distressed, I became so thankful to God... I kept thanking God for strengthening me so that I could support other people, family members who were really devastated. Someone later told me that God was inviting me to pray that night so my brother would not die! I replied that death is part of life and I strongly believe God was strengthening and empowering me to be able to cope with this second sudden death. A few days later, we learned that my brother had actually died between 8.00 pm and 9.00 pm the day before he was found, which coincided with the time the Lord was inviting me to pray. Yes, the Lord knows everything!

All this is to say, serving God does not replace spending time with Him. Now, to any aspiring servants of God, who does not know what to do in church, first learn to develop an intimate relationship with the Lord. As you do, allow the Spirit to show you an area where help and support are needed and start working in it, after getting the consent of your spiritual leader, of course. God will not give you responsibilities when you see some mess in the church, and you tend to wait for others to clean it. As I always ask people who criticise easily: why do you think God opened your eyes to see that paper on the floor that everyone else did not see? It was for *you* to pick it up, not for *you* to criticise the church for being dirty or for *you* to point your finger at the negligent cleaner or call them to come and clean it.

By becoming proactive in the house of God now, in due time, the Lord will confirm your calling or ministry. Stop therefore sitting down and pretending, 'I don't know what God wants me to do;' 'I don't know what's my calling.' Your calling is to witness about Jesus, starting in your surroundings, to try and bring all who still don't have a relationship with Him to get to know Him through your changed character and your displayed love. Your calling is also to help the work of God advance by supporting the church you attend to help spread the good news, without grumbling. Why?

Because the church is led by human beings who have limitations just like you, too. Now, you know where to start if you did not have an idea! As you do so, God will gradually develop your ministry.

Before being called myself, I was in a church where the pastor became a persecutor because God was using me to always bring order wherever I saw disorder in people's behaviour. I was not doing it directly but would always let him know so he could take biblical action, not knowing that he was using what I was telling him to bring church members to hate me and look down on me. Nevertheless, I did not leave that church and used to tell them, publicly, that nobody was going to discourage me enough for me to leave. I trusted that one day, God was going to create an opportunity to remove me from there. For more than seven months, I was subjected to gossip, disrespect from some members as well as the pastor who worked hard to undermine the gifts God was developing in me. In the midst of all that intimidation, I started receiving words of knowledge and prophecies that would come to pass within hours or weeks. When the messages were positive, the pastor said they were from God; when the messages did not please him, he said they were from the devil. Yet, God always confirmed all the messages were from Him.

During a Sunday service, this pastor showed his real motivation following my testimony about a friend of mine to whom I had given a prophecy, and it had come to pass a few months later, so he had blessed me with 1,000 euros. Hearing this, the pastor said that when I was blessed, he, the pastor was blessed because I was the only person in church who always gave a tithe to the nearest cent! I was appalled! Yet, all the time I stayed in that church, I did everything despite the ongoing suppression and oppression I was going through: whenever a need arose, I made it my personal issue because I was in the house of my loving Father. In other words, I did not look at what was happening in the church, so to speak. I was focusing on pleasing my Father in Heaven.

Believe it or not, two years after leaving that church, I thanked God as I realised that, my immersion for work in the ministry had taken place during that time of persecution where He had started humbling me to be able to serve Him. The Bible says we must die to self to become a bit more like Christ every day (Galatians 2:20-21). God knew the areas I needed to deny myself. And through this seemingly intimidating and quite unpleasant experience, He prepared me for ministry despite my lack of knowledge of His purposes and plans, which He started unfolding when the time came. How many people have never seen their ministry take shape, only because they have never allowed the pruning and the brokenness God wanted to do in them?

Indeed, our character can often be an obstacle to our ministry. Being willing to serve God is not enough. Even when we are available to minister, we truly need to be ready to take criticism, commit to making the sacrifices that come with serving. In short, as written in Matthew 16:24-26, be ready to deny yourself and take up your cross and follow Jesus.

To be brief, the Church of Christ must continue the work of salvation by spreading the Good News and setting the captives of the devil free, knowing that this will not happen by might, nor by power, but by the Spirit of God (see Zechariah 4:6). Thus, the urgency to teach the believers that the Holy Spirit's presence within them is not for them to start hearing from God or serving as ministers in the church, but to first convince them of their own sins through the hearing of the Word of God (see John 16:8). This will lead them to repentance and salvation, and then, help them to become useful for the Kingdom as their minds are renewed as the Bible says: *"...let the Spirit renew your thoughts and attitudes" (Ephesians 4:23, NLT).* That is what will empower them to become useful for the Kingdom.

Anointed for service

> *The Spirit of the Lord is on Me, because He has anointed Me to preach good news to the poor. He has sent Me to proclaim deliverance to the captives and recovery of sight to the blind, to release the oppressed, to proclaim the year of the Lord's favor (Luke 4:18-19).*

As mentioned previously concerning the early Church, whenever and wherever the resurrected Christ was preached, the Holy Spirit manifested and many people found deliverance and healing, instantly. When God was praised and worshipped, great miracles occurred. All that happened with or without the laying on hands, with or without fasting and prayers. What has changed since then? Though the Lord does not change, how come the Church has changed? Perhaps because we want to do things in our own understanding, we can't produce the fruit of the Spirit in the Church. And, if we can't produce the fruit of the Spirit, why expect the gifts of the Spirit to manifest, too?

Instead, many churches have developed a kind of voyeurism, which forces them to fake miracles sometimes or delude the children of God with promises of miracles, just because they do not know their real position in Christ. If God wants to do a miracle, He does not need to announce it a year before: He just does it! That's why it is called a miracle. If you start expecting a miracle, then it lessens the extraordinary and wonderful aspect of the divine a miracle should have. Experiencing miracles is commonplace in any local church that has allowed the Spirit of God to distribute or manifest the gift of miracles as was the case in the early church. However, there is a true concern when miracles now look more like the deeds of man, which promotes idolatry within the church. The Bible says we are to seek the Kingdom FIRST and the righteousness of God... and everything else, which includes miracles, shall be added to us.

Cornelius is our perfect example here. Without being a Christian, he was seeking the Kingdom and the righteousness of God. And God produced a miracle by allowing his conversion and that of his household. But how did this happen? Peter did not lay hands on them or pray for them. He only presented Jesus who died and was resurrected. That was enough to move the Holy Spirit who was obviously ready to act, seizing all of them who heard the Word spoken by Apostle Peter (see Acts 10:44). This passage shows us that the gospel is enough to change lives and circumstances.

Miracles should therefore not be at the centre of our focus in church or in our walk with Jesus. Focusing on miracles is a distraction that shows we have not matured or trusted God enough. Instead, we should focus on the miracle-maker, Jesus! Let's clarify this by demystifying one of the greatest distractions, or rather, the side-tracking of the devil, that is summed up in a very well-known expression: 'God told me…' So many people recall what God told them only when it comes to blessings, material possessions, well-being, breakthroughs or deliverance. Very few would tell you loud and clear that God says to quit sin or to renew their minds. The very fact that a believer only sees God's hand when everything is fine, and no wind is blowing against them is a sign of a misconception of who God is. This is to say that true repentance can be a miracle for someone who had been battling with sin for years.

Miracles are not only tangible as the believers have now reduced them to. Remember the great miracle that happened on the day of the Pentecost: nobody is recorded to have been healed or delivered from demons or else to receiving abundant material blessings that day. The wonderful miracle that occurred then was spiritual as three thousand souls were saved. The anointing present that day is what set all of them free from the captivity of the devil.

The main problem today is that, because there are mixed interpretations of what the anointing is, a great majority of people don't know that all Christians are anointed. Therefore, they follow 'anointed' servants of God to have them lay hands on them, break curses in their lives, and so on. Don't get me wrong: it is biblical to go to the elders to be laid hands on, anointed when sick or prayed for when needed. The practice that is not biblical is total dependence on ministers for what we could do ourselves. The Bible says:

> *Now it is God who makes both us and you stand firm in Christ. He anointed us, set his seal of ownership on us, and put his Spirit in our hearts as a deposit, guaranteeing what is to come (2 Corinthians 1:21– 22).*

Once, I attended a church meeting and on returning to my hotel, I had to pray to God in repentance because people were literally taking my hand to lay on themselves or rubbing their handkerchiefs on me because, for them, I was 'anointed' because a pastoral couple who had had difficulty conceiving were expecting a child since I had prayed for them during my previous visit. Anyway, I felt so bad that I prayed for the Lord to have mercy on us. Where does such idolatry take us, if not out of the power of God itself? Today, let the truth be told: if you keep looking up to the Spirit of God for a miracle in your life, it is because you have not yet understood that you already have exactly what are looking for.

Bondage and sinful habits can affect everyone's life, especially when they give us a guilty conscience. Many people try different things and approaches that may soothe their conscience, but the roots must be broken for us to be totally free. The only remedy that can offer lasting freedom is obeying the Word of God and walking by the Spirit! Unfortunately, when people feel bad about themselves, they hope that prayer is enough. Also, know that nobody can ever give you a good conscience: you need to do this part on your own! Remember that none of the apostles ever claimed to be 'anointed' for people to follow them. They all pointed people back to Jesus because they knew that the anointing we, the believers of Christ, have received comes from Him; therefore, it does not run out and continues to operate when all biblical conditions are met for it to flow:

> *I am writing these things to you about those who are trying to lead you astray. As for you, the anointing you received from him remains in you, and you do not need anyone to teach you. But as his anointing teaches you about all*

Let us, therefore, remember that the true biblical anointing is the one that yokes us to Jesus. And that, all Christians have already received as stated on the passage above. So, we need to start believing that we are truly redeemed and all we need to do is to walk in the Spirit to see all we have received in Christ manifest in us and through us, for the glory of God. This is essential in this time and age, because when we cannot discern right from wrong, how can we have the genuine anointing?

The reason why many believers are in confusion about the anointing is therefore linked to the Word of God that is preached to them or what they hear, since many like to self-feed through the Internet… and, unfortunately, many churches have forsaken teaching the truth, preferring teaching what itches people's ears. Obviously, solid teaching of the Word protects believers and enables them to recognize the false anointing by the power of the Holy Spirit. So it is not biblical for people to follow men or go to a church for more anointing because the Holy Spirit who is the anointing is already living in us to lead us to the truth, to God's Word and point us to Jesus Christ, nothing or no one else, but Jesus.

Chapter IV
No Fear in War

Many believers are paralysed by fear but will not admit it because we are taught that fear and doubt are the enemies of faith. It is always easier to look for excuses or scapegoats to avoid the reality of tackling our fears, especially when we experience failure or plans being thwarted. As a result, we try to hide our weakened faith by reciting the Scriptures as if they have a magical effect when voiced. Now, acknowledging our fear is not showing we are weak. In fact, knowing the root of our fear could be a great asset for us to defeat the enemy.

Worry – the root of fear

Worry is persistent fear that gives a greater advantage to the devil in spiritual warfare. Most of the time, our worries do take root over the very things God is asking us not to worry about:

> *Therefore, I tell you, do not worry about your life, what you will eat or drink; or about your body, what you will wear. Is not life more than food, and the body more than clothes? Look at the birds of the air; they do not sow or reap or store away in barns, and yet your heavenly Father feeds them. Are you not much more valuable than they? Can any one of you by worrying add a single hour to your life? "And why do you worry about clothes? See how the flowers of the field grow. They do not labor or spin. Yet I tell you that not even Solomon in all his splendor was dressed like one of these. If that is how God clothes the grass of the field, which is here today and tomorrow is*

Consider toddlers, who are daring and usually fearless until they hurt. Even when they experience a distressing event such as falling as they are learning to walk, it does not stop them from trying again because their subconscious has not developed a negative response towards walking. In contrast, adults would intentionally distance themselves from similar circumstances since they don't want to take the risk of being hurt again. Children will never tell you that they know how it feels to hurt when falling, but adults will detail every hurt of the past, sometimes with vivid words, as if that past event just happened. Recollection of the past can sometimes be very painful, making it hard for us to be able to pray, fast or move forward. When the soul is always wrestling with doubts or fear, living a victorious, abundant life is impossible. That is the reason why it is not unusual to hear that people who have everything that money could buy end up committing suicide.

Jesus taught that fear reveals the level of our faith. He spoke about this to His disciples when they panicked in the face of the storm:

In this passage, Jesus rebukes His disciples for being fearful about their safety even in His presence. Because such rebuke comes from the Lord directly, it sounds acceptable. Who can imagine if this reaction were not directly from Jesus?

Sometimes, figuratively, we are in a sinking boat out at sea and we hear people (family members, friends or pastors) telling us not to be afraid: 'Things will work out in the long run.' That's when we usually protest, 'I know my situation better than you!' The fact is, we are sometimes too conscious of our unwanted circumstances and the anxious thoughts built around them. Yet, the only way to unravel situations that are entangled because of these thoughts is changing them by using the Word of God. Even the world has understood that only positive thinking can help people out of some anxiety issues. We are not to imitate the world, but trust that the Word provides the right method for us to change our thought life.

Changing our thought life

One way to move towards a victorious life is to avoid rehearsing hurtful episodes of our lives. Every difficulty is like a step to move forward towards our godly purposes, with our eyes set on Jesus. Remember that He, too, experienced overwhelming fear and doubt when He was faced with the Cross: *"And being in anguish, he prayed more earnestly, and his sweat was like drops of blood falling to the ground"* (Luke 22:44). When we feel anxious, we often become so disheartened and miserable that we don't pray as we should. Jesus did just the opposite. He prayed more earnestly until He received help from Heaven.

This also confirms what Jesus says in Matthew 6:34: *"...do not worry about tomorrow, for tomorrow will worry about itself. Each day has enough trouble of its own."* Fear not only kills faith, but it also keeps us far away from our godly purposes and opens the door to the devil to lead us to despair when things look unattainable.

Changing our thought life is also to stop being suspicious of everyone and everything: a glass falls on the floor does not necessarily mean a ghost or an evil spirit is in your house; someone looking at you does not mean they are planning evil against you; being single does not necessarily mean that you are cursed or a spiritual spouse is stopping you from getting married. Apostle Paul never married but was made whole again by Christ who used him powerfully despite his state! Being barren or not being able to carry a pregnancy through does not necessarily mean that a demon is behind it. The Bible says, *"the Lord had closed Hannah's womb"* (1 Samuel 1:6). Many things happen to us every day, THAT God ALLOWS! How can we always confess that God is in control, yet refuse to accept the truth? The Bible says:

Who can speak and have it happen if the Lord has not decreed it? Is it not from the mouth of the Most High that both calamities and good things come? Why should the living complain when punished for their sins? Let us examine our ways and test them, and let us return to the Lord (Lamentations 3:37-40).

Job lost everything: possessions and children! When such a thing happens nowadays, most people, especially in Africa, attribute them directly to all the witches in the village as if it is not normal to have an accident, to fall sick or die. An African saying even says 'if someone dies in weird conditions, an acquaintance was involved.' Does that mean there is no evil around? Certainly not. But, let's not give more control to the devil than he actually has. Yes, he has power, but not the might to decide on or have the last word in anybody's life: *"The days of humans are determined; you have decreed the number of their months and have set limits they cannot exceed" (Job 14:5)*. Yes, only God has the power to shorten or prolong our lives: *"Go and tell Hezekiah, 'This is what the LORD, the God of your father David, says: I have heard your prayer and seen your tears; I will add fifteen years to your life'"* *(Isaiah 38:5)*. So instead of nurturing evil thoughts that do us no good other than isolating us in a mental prison, we should say like the psalmist: *"into your hands I commit my spirit; deliver me, Lord, my faithful God" (Psalm 31:5)*. Blaming, pointing fingers for all that happens to us is just the best way to nurture fear in our minds.

Indeed, fear can distort our minds and we can become so blinded, even agents of the devil himself, so much that, instead of accusing us before God, he can even begin to justify himself! We are not fighting against flesh and blood... Satan can distract each of us to accomplish his destructive agendas in our families, our work, our relationships or our church. The only remedy is to seek God in a church that preaches the full gospel and walk in the Word.

Likewise, when our thinking is far from the Word, we begin to judge everyone we meet. Remember that Jesus sat with thieves, but He never judged or rejected them. He knew that Judas was stealing the offerings (John 12:6), but because He was grace among men, He accepted everyone without exception. People are free to refuse or reject His grace, yet it is real. Therefore, changing our thoughts is surely a way to win the difficult battle of the mind that can enslave us in a prison that no one but us has the keys to open; and this key begins with the firm decision to stop being suspicious, stop judging everything in our environment and everyone except ourselves. Yes, something may have happened to you in the past that may have led you to such captive thoughts. But today is a new day, you have received renewed mercy... decide to change so the Spirit can help you; thus, you will see deliverance in your thought life!

Gideon's battle with fear

We can learn a lot about dealing with fear from the lessons God taught to Gideon. When God wanted to give victory to Gideon over the Midianites, He had to prepare Gideon for battle by empowering him. He had to first teach him how to deal with fear (see Judges 6 and 7). The key was to trust in Him implicitly and not in his human reasoning. The first thing He did was to ask him to select the people who were going to go to battle with him. Then God began to systematically short-list them. Those who behaved carelessly were sent back home. Why so? Because God wanted us to learn that winning a great battle does not depend on the number of people supporting or following us.

God will not give us a task or a mission if we cannot handle it spiritually or physically, but we must be ready for surprises. In Gideon's case, having 32,000 men for the great battle seemed the right PHYSICAL choice as the enemy's army numbered more than 135,000 men (Judges 8:10). Yet, the physical does not prevail over the spiritual, which is why God had to intervene. The Lord said to Gideon:

> *"You have too many men. I cannot deliver Midian into their hands, or Israel would boast against me, 'My own strength has saved me.' Now announce to the army, 'Anyone who trembles with fear may turn back and leave Mount Gilead.'" So, twenty-two thousand men left, while ten thousand remained (Judges 7:2-3).*

God said to Gideon to eliminate those who 'tremble with fear'. Oftentimes, we stick with friends who spend time criticising us, undermining us, discouraging us or projecting their own insecurities on to us. God is clearly advising us that those who are fearful of our big projects, our big challenges or battles will, in the end, turn their back and leave the mountain out of their own fears. So, let go of them!

Certainly, Gideon was counting on his sizeable army to help him accomplish his divine assignment. Now, after eliminating the faint-hearted, his army was decreased to about 10,000 men. This was already a huge shock for Gideon. But God, who knows everything, knew many were still not fit enough for war. He told Gideon to offer them refreshment by the river. There, the real character of the great majority came out:

> *But the LORD said to Gideon, "There are still too many men. Take them down to the water, and I will thin them out for you there. If I say, 'This one shall go with you,' he shall go; but if I say, 'This one shall not go with you,' he shall not go." So, Gideon took the men down to the water. There the LORD told him, "Separate those who lap the water with their tongues as a dog laps from those who kneel down to drink." Three hundred of them drank from cupped hands, lapping like dogs. All the rest got down on their knees to drink. The LORD said to Gideon, "With the three hundred men that lapped I will save you and give the Midianites into your hands. Let all the others go home." So, Gideon sent the rest of the Israelites home but kept the three hundred, who took over the provisions and trumpets of the others. Now the camp of Midian lay below him in the valley (Judges 7:4-8).*

Let's note this: God first let Gideon choose his own army. Why? Because He had to first entrust Gideon with practical things to see if the latter would allow his will to be aligned with His. Gideon did what God had told him by ordering the soldiers who were scared to go back home (Judges 7:3). Fear is deadlier than the enemy's bullet because it can cause long term effects and kill an individual's soul. Going to war with fearful people would jeopardise the entire mission and the missionaries. Now, God Himself took control of the rest, whittling down the army to less than 1% of the original number. This was the calibre of the soldiers who had the heart and the mind to stand with Gideon in battle.

Why did God choose Gideon, despite his fears and doubts, as expressed in Judges 6:15? And, to make things worse, why did He downsize Gideon's army? Because God does not look at the way we see ourselves, but what He is doing in our character. He saw in Gideon a *"mighty warrior" (Judges 6:12)*. Isn't it interesting, that Gideon was initially hiding from the same Midianites that God would send him to fight? Why did God have to choose the weakest man from the weakest clan? Because of the transforming power of God's Word when we cooperate with Him! What made Gideon mighty before God was his obedience. In other words, Gideon was qualified by his awe at the presence of God and the calling to save Israel, not his knowledge of the Scriptures or any known skill. In short, Gideon was qualified by his choice to lean on God's strength and grace, rather than on his own understanding.

So, the message for us today is that God can use any one of us who trusts in Him despite our shortcomings. For He says to us: *"My grace is sufficient for you, for My power is made perfect in weakness" (2 Corinthians 12:9)*. However, instead of humbling ourselves as Gideon did, very often, once God calls us to do a task, we are guilty of starting off without Him, priding ourselves in being qualified based on our natural abilities. With Gideon, we see that, after giving him the mission, God continued to give him instruction after instruction so that he would totally rely on Him for strategy. In spite of all that, still uncertain of the Lord's dependability, Gideon had to ask God for signs as an assurance that He was with him:

> *Gideon replied, "If now I have found favor in your eyes, give me a sign that it is really you talking to me. Please do not go away until I come back and bring my offering and set it before you."*
> *And the Lord said, "I will wait until you return."*
> *Gideon went inside, prepared a young goat, and from an ephah of flour he made bread without yeast. Putting the meat in a basket and its broth in a pot, he brought them out and offered them to him under the oak (Judges 6:17-19).*

Gideon himself decided to give an offering to God because he was thankful that he had found favour in God's eyes! AND THE LORD WAITED FOR IT! When you find favour in the eyes of God, what is the next thing you do? Nowadays, the tendency is to wait to be asked to give an offering, call our loved ones or post pictures to share our joy on social media! But here, we learn that God waited for Gideon's offering. Gideon applied a simple principle of God: GIVING! And the Bible later tells us that God did exactly what Gideon asked Him: He not only gave Gideon the needed signs to alleviate his fears (Judges 6:39-40) but also led him to the promised success:

> *Now the camp of Midian lay below him in the valley. During that night the Lord said to Gideon, "Get up, go down against the camp, because I am going to give it into your hands. If you are afraid to attack, go down to the camp with your servant Purah and listen to what they are saying. Afterward, you will be encouraged to attack the camp." So, he and Purah his servant went down to the outposts of the camp (Judges 7:8-11).*

God had a strategy and He gave it to Gideon because he maintained close communication with Him and took his marching orders from the Lord. He did not try to work things out on his own.

Fear is a learnt phenomenon

Fear is not natural to man; it is taught to us from childhood. It imposes itself on you through external factors always standing at the door between you and the thing you desire. That is why almost every book of the Bible tells us: 'Do not be afraid!' For every situation we go through, God says: 'Fear not!' He is with us, He will fight for us, He is going with us. Our Creator knows that fear has a power that stems from the unknown. Indeed, we don't always know, nor are we sure what will happen if calamity strikes because we don't have control of the future. In some cases, fear can sneak in on our mind, leading us to withdraw, hide, fail or even be defeated.

No wonder the Lord commands us 365 times in the Bible (one for each day) not to be fearful of what we don't know! How many people start worrying at not being able to pay the bills at the start of the month and are sometimes surprised that God has made a way where there seemed to be none! Jesus told us to cast our anxieties on Him so that we do not have to carry those heavy burdens and fear unknown outcomes.

Fear breeds many evils

When God created man and placed him in the garden of Eden, man was walking naked, unashamed (Genesis 2:25). The same man walked without fear around the fierce lions or the strongest animals; nothing could cause him to hide. He walked in authority because his Father had given him dominion over all of nature, and all these animals had to obey and submit to him. It is important to remember this because it is the key to understanding the root cause of fear in man. Once Adam and Eve sinned, their first reflex was to hide when they heard God looking for them. Their experience of fear was linked to the discovery that they were naked:

> *Then the eyes of both of them were opened, and they realized they were naked; so, they sewed fig leaves*

together and made coverings for themselves. Then the man and his wife heard the sound of the Lord God as he was walking in the garden in the cool of the day, and they hid from the Lord God among the trees of the garden. But the Lord God called to the man, "Where are you?" He answered, "I heard you in the garden, and I was afraid because I was naked; so, I hid" (Genesis 3:7-10).

Genesis 3:7 tells us that as soon as they realised that they were naked, they tried to cover themselves with fig leaves. The voice of their Creator caused them to feel ashamed and hide. Thus, we know Satan had already worked his evil character into them, causing them to fear the One with whom they had such close fellowship when they were not conscious of their nakedness!

Indeed, fear comes from the devil and breeds many more evils so that we try to hide from the God who sees and knows everything. What Adam and Eve were trying to hide from God, over and above their physical nudity was their spiritual nakedness caused by their rebellion. Remember that in Genesis 2:17, God had given them a clear instruction: *"...you must not eat from the tree of the knowledge of good and evil, for when you eat from it you will certainly die."* This makes more sense to understand why they were now afraid, doesn't it? They were now out of God's will; they were spiritually dead. Now that they were naked, they lost their peace… fear had taken the place of their inner peace… so they hid from God.

All the time Adam and Eve were in the garden of God, walking by His Word, they never were afraid of anything. So, when does fear creep in? From the moment they moved out of God's protective covering! Their spiritual position as the keepers of the garden of Eden changed when they were stripped of that authority and the devil took over control. At once, they became conscious of their nakedness, their vulnerability and their embarrassment at being exposed. This led to fear and the instinct to escape. And that is what most of us do: we work hard at trying to conceal our fears instead of confronting them so we can get rid of them. In fact, discovering the deep causes of our fear is paramount to overcoming it because fear is always triggered by a lie about our situation, ourselves or our surroundings. The Bible tells us that lies are perpetuated by the devil and *"when he lies, he speaks his native language, for he is a liar and the father of lies" (John 8:44)*. Thus, just as he deceived Adam and Eve, leading them to be afraid and hide, the devil can deceive us. When we entertain his lies, fear settles in our minds to start producing evil thoughts, despair, distrust and isolation.

Overcoming fear

The key to overcoming fear of any kind is found in the Word of God: *"as he thinks in his heart, so is he" (Proverbs 23:7)*. What is in your heart concerning your life, your health, your situation, the people around you? Jesus came to set the captives free. When we nurture fear, we pave the way to bondage in our lives. It is therefore important to always remember that we can choose to resist fear in every circumstance (James 4:7).

Praying to God for fear to leave us is not exercising faith and that will change absolutely nothing. But, showing God that we are standing on His Word is much more powerful than any prayer since the battle of the mind is in its ability to identify the force ruling our thoughts: faith or fear? The Word of God or the lies of the devil? Many people want to get rid of their fears using a band-aid to bandage the surface. But Jesus offered the solution through the work of the Cross to demolish those strongholds of deception: *"The weapons we fight with are not the weapons of the world. On the contrary, they have divine power to demolish strongholds"* (2 Corinthians 10:4).

Having established that fear comes from lies, *"We demolish arguments and every pretension that sets itself up against the knowledge of God, and we take captive every thought to make it obedient to Christ"* (2 Corinthians 10:5). When every one of our thoughts is submitted to the lordship of Jesus Christ, and we begin to take down every lie of the enemy, then we will begin to experience freedom, peace, joy and success in our lives.

Now, you may wonder where you should start. The answer is simple: find out what God says about you in His Word. Find in it the solution that Jesus has created for you. Finally, use the truth you find to *"take captive every thought"* that has been holding you hostage. Remember, God wants you to regain the control you have lost to the devil's lies. Ensure that your thoughts are lined up with the Word of God, no matter what happens, and believe that victory has been made available to you through the finished work of Jesus Christ.

Chapter V
When Nothing Seems to Work...

We all like life to move smoothly, with realistic challenges that encourage us to push through our limits. However, we also need to tackle many undesirable situations from time to time. The way we welcome, deal with or react to them can give an unexpected turn to our lives: win or lose!

Natural instincts

When driving on a winding road, not knowing what is ahead of the bend, every reasonable driver would slow down. This is something we learn at a driving school, and even our natural instincts will urge us to slow down to avoid a crash. We are motivated by the thought of imminent danger from the hidden side of the road.

Likewise, our circumstances can sometimes become so unpredictable and out of control that nothing, but failure seems impending. In such situations, it is wise to walk with caution and seek to know what God sees ahead of the bend. God created us with limitations, so we need the input and knowledge of others, sometimes, to give us the broader picture. Some people walk through life based on their own knowledge and intuition that often lead them into danger. Let's be straightforward: you don't know everything about your life and stop thinking that the only way God can talk to you is directly to you. Most of the time, He will speak to you through His Word, circumstances or people.

Our *natural* instinct is not a *spiritual* instinct. Trusting and believing in our natural instincts can become detrimental when we tend to worry, for instance. In Jeremiah 17:9, the Bible tells us that *"The heart is deceitful above all things and beyond cure. Who can understand it?"* In fact, we are warned that the people who follow their natural instincts are following their ungodly desires:

> *They said to you, "In the last times there will be scoffers*
> *who will follow their own ungodly desires." These are the*
> *people who divide you, who follow mere natural instincts*
> *and do not have the Spirit (Jude 1:18-19).*

Sometimes we do say we heard God's guidance or direction. Today, let me ask you a question. How do you know for sure that it is God, and not your natural instinct, that is guiding you? This answer is easy: if you have not sought God first for guidance or direction, it is most likely that you are going by your instinct. Now, when you have sought the Lord, knowing Bible verses is not necessarily a sign that God agrees with the direction or guidance you think you have found, because we can actually find Bible verses that are tailored to our desires. And this applies to the online preaching we choose to listen to as if we are choosing an entertaining book on a library shelf. Such preaching is good for our spiritual development, but not necessarily an answer from God to you. Therefore, the most important thing to help us distinguish between our natural instincts and the will of God remains the inner witness of the Spirit of God in us. He will always lead us to do what is right for God.

A mind divided

When nothing seems to work in our lives, we tend to look for external reasons: our past, our past mistakes, our family background or obstacles that could have come against our success. Now, there is a greater factor that is summed up by the verse: *"If a house is divided against itself, that house cannot stand" (Mark 3:25).* This Scripture is speaking about each one of us who are the dwelling place of the Holy Spirit! Many people are double minded within themselves, which leads them in circles. How can they stand?

A great number of believers do not understand the power of the church established by Christ. How can they stand as Christians? Wearing combat trousers and carrying a gun does not make anyone a solider unless they trained for many years and have been validated in their role. And we know the strict discipline, endurance, allegiance to their country, sacrifice of living away from family and friends for prolonged periods that soldiers have to endure. So, how is it that many believers, just by reading the Bible, think they can impudently call themselves soldiers for Christ? When you mention what they need to sacrifice, they mention the grace of God, forgetting that Jesus said we all have to carry our cross to follow Him and we have to lay down our burdens at His feet.

Some believers are so bogged down with the burdens of their past, that they cannot have a conversation for five minutes without going back there. When our actions do not match our thoughts, our house is divided internally. In fact, when nothing works in our lives, we should go back to Jeremiah 29:11 and remind ourselves that God has a purpose, hope and a future for us. It's not about the way we perceive our present situation but about confidence in God's work in us. In fact, it is in the most trying of times that we should show our loyalty to God, like Job who asked his wife during the hardest period of his life, in Job 2:10: *"Shall we accept good from God, and not trouble?"*

All things work for good

We need to learn that God takes care of us even when we are not aware of His presence: *"Be strong and courageous. Do not be afraid or terrified because of them, for the Lord your God goes with you; he will never leave you nor forsake you"* (Deuteronomy 31:6). How much trust do we put in these words?

The main problem is that we like to bargain with the Word of God when we experience setbacks. Now, let us remember that the Resurrection of Christ happened after Jesus had died, not before.

This means we need to go through hardship before God can resurrect us because He is the initiator of the Resurrection. Just as defeat seemed obvious on the Cross, this sense of defeat is something we, too, have to experience. The difference is that we know the end will be victorious for us in Christ. Therefore, wondering why bad things happen to us despite God being with us is a vain question: evil is on earth and the only way to escape hardship is to fall asleep for eternity. Remember that no matter what you are going through, *"in all things God works for the good of those who love him, who have been called according to his purpose" (Romans 8:28)*.

Now, the Bible tells us many times of the necessity to move on, move forward and see the way open up. To respond with such confidence, our character must first be trained and equipped. Nobody can say how they would always react in a difficult situation, because our reactions depend on the mood of the day, our general inner state and how stressful the situation is. However, when we learn to live a godly life and choose to *"rejoice always, pray continually, give thanks in all circumstances" (1 Thessalonians 5:16-18)*, that can make a huge difference in our reaction to undesirable situations. And, a godly mindset also knows that God uses such situations to strengthen our faith and perseverance in Him. We become aware that His perfect timing sometimes requires patience and self-control. We should therefore always remind ourselves that we are not alone in our battles, and God is capable of creating a whole new reality for us out of absolutely nothing:

> *Through faith we understand that the worlds were framed by the word of God, so that things which are seen were not made of things which do appear (Hebrews 11:3).*

Once again, it is through faith expressed in hardship that God can create a way in the wilderness. Job never lost faith in God's action even when he lost his possessions and his children. Maybe he was conscious that all he had belonged to God:

> *The heavens are yours, and yours also the earth; you founded the world and all that is in it (Psalm 89:11);*

> *The earth is the Lord's, and everything in it, the world, and all who live in it (Psalm 24:1);*

> *But remember the Lord your God, for it is he who gives you the ability to produce wealth, and so confirms his covenant, which he swore to your ancestors, as it is today (Deuteronomy 8:18);*

> *Children are a heritage from the Lord, offspring a reward from him (Psalm 127:3).*

Let's give ownership back to God

When we stop thinking that all is ours, then we would stop enslaving ourselves to work so hard to obtain wealth, riches or security. The devil's rule in this present age does not remove the fact that God is the owner of everything. So, when nothing works right, we should turn to Him instead of trying to run away and sort things out as we often do.

Whenever people question why their world is going so wrong while there is a God, they never actually ask themselves if they have tried to deprive God of His exclusive ownership of their lives. Sin, sufferings and death entered the world because of Adam and Eve's original disobedience to God. Once and for all, let us resolve that God is above every adverse situation we may go through, whether failing health, financial issues or oppression.

In brief, unless we make the firm decision to stop trying when nothing seems to work, we will continue fighting against the wind or confronting the problem in our own strength until we are worn out. The enemy does not want us to be in a position to fight back. So, it's crucial for every believer to understand that, when nothing seems to work when nothing seems to move forward, the first thing to do is actually to... stop! Yes, stop doing what you have been doing and calmly assess the situation!

One night I was driving home from visiting a friend and I did not know my way back as I was trying a new route. I managed to get halfway until I became unsure of the road. I stopped my car, prayed to ask the Spirit of God (my Helper) to guide me from where I was. I boldly resumed driving, still not sure of my way. Before I knew it, I drove to a street I recognised, and from there I could confidently drive home.

So, when nothing works, stop first. Nothing can be improved when we are in confusion, delusion or in a mess. We always expect God to meet us in our mess. He may do that. But most of the time, He will wait for us to be fed up of our mess and return to Him before He starts helping us. Remember the prodigal son! The father let him be where he was, eating with pigs. He waited until he came back home.

Jesus is always on time and never abandons us in our difficult moments. Perhaps it is just because we are busy trying to fix things that we cannot see or hear Him. Remember the story of Martha in Luke 10:41-42? Jesus did not think that the sister who dropped everything to listen to Him was wasting her time. In fact, He said that the one who continued being busy, trying to do good was anxious. And the problem with anxiety is that it can create unwanted feelings in us such as fear, jealousy, insecurity. So, stop! Whatever area of your life is affected right now is not too high or too wide for the Lord not to address. He only wants the space to enter and get you out of it. As simple as this seems, this is also one of the most difficult battles for many people because they have grown the leech habit in their mind. They deceive themselves that things can be well done only with their input; the world can be better only with their presence. They make themselves so central to everything, even when they are not needed, but they forget that *"we can do nothing without Christ" (John 15:5)*. Christ is the one who needs to be in the midst of all situations, not us!

Some steps to take

When the boat was threatening to sink, the disciples called on Jesus, who was fast asleep, and He rebuked them for their lack of faith. So when nothing seems to work, the first thing to do is stop fighting demons, stop turning back to the paralysing past that is gradually killing you by turning you into a pillar of salt, stop pointing fingers at people, stop accusing God of being an agent of the devil, stop lying to yourself but be willing to check the state of your faith in the Lord. Obviously, the faith that brought you to accept Him as your Lord and Saviour is the same faith you need to depend on Him in times of hardship. The only difference is that now, you must grow your faith to abandon yourself to His lordship and let Him hold your hands to take you through that storm.

When asked to stop bad habits, we have excuses, justifications or don't understand. That's why it's important to stop... until we become willing, available and ready. Why would anybody keep driving to a destination when they do not know the way?

If your spiritual life has shifted from a lively zeal and thirst to a monotonous routine, pausing will stop you blaming the church's programme or your pastor's preaching or any other external reason for your spiritual setback. God promises to help us through every situation, but we need to learn to check ourselves first – that's being WILLING to move forward. Then we need to check our inner development – that's being AVAILABLE; and, finally, we need to allow change to take place – that's being READY to win the battle.

Chapter VI
Keys to Success in War

When you are cooking and you run out of salt, you have two choices: run to the store or ask your neighbour – that is, if you are on good terms with them. These two examples have a common starting point: a need. When we have a prayer need, do we ask and expect to see God provide for that need? Do we exercise enough faith to be able to see Him fulfilling His promises? Do we rest in the assurance of those promises happening? Or do we fret and worry?

> *...do not worry about your life, what you will eat or drink; or about your body, what you will wear. Is not life more than food, and the body more than clothes? Look at the birds of the air; they do not sow or reap or store away in barns, and yet your heavenly Father feeds them (Matthew 6:25-33).*

God gives us further assurance of His provision by saying, *"I am watching to see that my word is fulfilled" (Jeremiah 1:12).* Knowing this, we, on our part, must see that we have fulfilled two conditions He has set for that promise to work out:

> ***So do not worry***, *saying, 'What shall we eat?' or 'What shall we drink?' or 'What shall we wear?' For the pagans run after all these things, and your heavenly Father knows that you need them. But **seek first his kingdom** and his righteousness, and all these things will be given to you as well (Matthew 6:31-33, emphasis added).*

The two conditions are: STOP WORRYING and MAKE KINGDOM BUSINESS your priority.

When we need something and want God to provide for it, the only thing that could hamper God's action is the fact that we are not seeking first His righteousness and not making His Kingdom business our priority. Most of the time, we want God to provide first, and then we align ourselves with what He says. But that is not exercising faith, as faith is to believe or act when we have not seen the outcome! It is easier for any of us to kneel down to ask God to answer a prayer for His provision for the things we need. But do we ever question the effectiveness of the way we pray?

Pray out of relationship

The Bible says to pray every time and for everything – but not anyhow! When a problem arises, it is good to get down to prayer. However, only some prayers are answered by God: prayers that are according to His will and depending on the way we approach Him. Most of us would pray just like we would head to the shop to buy some salt because that involves a quick transaction, which we can do independently without cultivating a relationship with anyone. Is that the way we would pray for God to meet our need? Do we also want a quick transaction which we can do independently without knowing Him, our Provider?

Remember that prayer is about communicating with God who hears us and speaks to us when we come to Him. It is about building a relationship. It is not about going to a shop and presenting Him with a 'shopping list'. When you pray out of relationship rather than out of transaction, you already have your answer.

In March 2018, I was preparing to travel to India and to Ghana. I had just bought my plane ticket for India, which was the double of the price I expected. I knew it was God's will for me to travel, so there was no need asking God HOW I was going to pay for the second trip. One morning, during my prayer time, I asked the Lord: 'WHO is going to pay for my next trip to Ghana?' That very evening, God provided for my trip through a sister in our church who had received a refund voucher from an airplane company and decided to offer it to me. God had answered me because I had asked Him a question in faith, that was not questioning the possibility for me to travel. For me, I was going to travel, and someone had to provide the ticket. Also, note that my prayer was quite precise. How often do we miss the point with our 'shopping list' prayers and God is looking at us thinking: 'What exactly do you want me to do?'

Sometimes too, we have many bills to pay and when someone (a child, for example) uses more than we expected, we shout at them: 'Who is going to pay?' The Bible tells us not to worry, for our Provider is the one who owns the silver and gold, and the cattle on a thousand hills. Most people don't receive because they don't ask God in faith. They ask in a worried and trembling voice. Faith gives us the assurance that God will answer us one way or another. When you ask God without faith, the next thing you will do is DO something, like fasting, going to church more than normal or reading your dusty Bible... or use the best tool in our ready-made culture: Google or YouTube where we look for preaching on how to get our prayer answered. This is spiritual bribery that deceives no one but yourself.

When you ask God in faith, you will WAIT on Him, too. Standing in the way of God's action will never speed up that action. Let us bear in mind that God in Heaven has no earthly needs as we do. So, if we want our needs to be met by Him, we must apply His rules. A 'shopping list' prayer can't be answered by God, because everything on our shopping list is not necessary or beneficial for us. If you pray for something you can sort out yourself, why do you bother presenting it to God then? He does not share His glory!

So, when you need salt, present your request precisely to God instead of first trying to buy it because that shows you have the means to get it from another source than God. These tendencies have made us independent of God, making us turn to Him only when our efforts to sort things out have failed. Yet, the Word says: *"**in everything** you do, **put God first**, and he will direct you and crown your efforts with success (Proverbs 3:6, TLB, emphasis added)*.

Knowing all this brings us to the crucial realisation that, when we seek God for something other than Himself, we may never know what He wants for us. When we stop pushing our requests, demands and must-do lists to His throne, then He starts listening to us. The truth must be told: not every prayer reaches the throne-room of God!

> *And when you pray, do not keep on babbling like pagans, for they think they will be heard because of their many words (Matthew 6:7).*

We need to stop crying out to God in vain: our circumstances do not move God because He knows what is happening in our lives anyway. The Bible says: *"Do not be like them, for your Father knows what you need before you ask him" (Matthew 6:8).* All God wants to see in us is our will being abandoned to His, and faith that moves mountains arising. How many times have we tried to move mountains on our own strength or our tears, our mouths, our fists, our minds? Jesus said: faith as little as a mustard seed moves mountains. Nothing else!

Be strategic in prayer

Many people watched *War Room*, a movie that shows us that you can't win a war without sitting down to sketch a battle plan. Being in a hurry to see God's move that gives us victory still requires proper planning. We have already mentioned it: our God does not work out of confusion, for He is a God of order. Therefore, whenever we are oppressed or spiritually attacked, starting to pray or fast does not always guarantee victory, or should I say, at least the way we expect.

A few years back, I was contacted by someone who was facing prison just a month before their sentencing. We prayed and fasted, and I told the person from the beginning that, doing so, did not mean that they would inevitably escape prison. Though they ended up going to prison, God's favour and hand were upon them throughout the period and even their sentence was commuted for good behaviour. Later, after one or two years, this young person acknowledged that going to prison had, in fact, spared them because it was God's way to get them out of much greater problems. God knows our future. He answers our prayers the way that fits His plans and purposes for that future, not necessarily the way we might have designed them, in keeping with the way we expect to be answered.

In a crisis, everyone primarily looks for a quick fix to stop the pain. Applying a patch on a leaking hole would not stop the flood in your house! That's what emergency prayers and fasting do in times of crisis. Yes, you can feel peace and even feel victorious, but it won't last because we tend to forget that when the enemy is on our case, he takes time by prowling around us until he finds an opening for attack. According to an online dictionary, 'prowling' means *"moving around quietly in a place trying not to be seen or heard, such as an animal does when hunting."* A hungry animal will not stop until the targeted prey is exhausted or killed. So, how can we expect to counter the attacks of the enemy with irregular quick-fix prayers and fasting?

If we do not move from the quest for a quick fix to the search for lasting solutions that can only be given by the Lord, it is mostly because of our weak faith in Him. The Bible says, *"Don't give the devil any opportunity to work" (Ephesians 4:27, GW).* Indeed, we should defend ourselves when needed, but we should also retaliate when attacked because the enemy will not flee unless we resist him (James 4:7). For that, we need to be prepared. No soldier goes to war without having a battle strategy. If you don't know why the enemy is attacking a certain area of your life, how can you even pray for that area? We have hints: the enemy attacks us where we are most vulnerable. What makes you vulnerable? If you don't know yourself enough, the devil knows and will use those moments of weakness to get in and attack you.

We are at war against evil forces. To win the battle, we must hold fast to our victory in Christ. How? By acknowledging that we don't have to start our fight from scratch: we are already seated in heavenly places with the Lord and all demonic powers are under our feet. Thus, we organise our battle from that position of victory... If you are wallowing in self-pity, can you see that the enemy is trying out a new trick? Certainly not, because your teary eyes won't allow you to see what's happening. Similarly, if you are fighting the enemy to obtain something already yours in Christ, your efforts are in vain. Sometimes, claiming back what is yours is enough. All this is to say that not knowing how to fight owing to the lack of a strategy is worse because we waste our energy, our confidence and our knowledge.

Once discouraged because we have tried different kinds of prayers, different approaches to tackling the problems we face, we can only stand defeated before the enemy. Are you presently thinking you have tried everything, but nothing worked? Perhaps the time has come for you to do one simple thing: stop standing and return to the position where every strategy comes from, in the heavenly realm! Let's look closely at what the Scriptures say:

> *Praise be to the God and Father of our Lord Jesus Christ, who has blessed us in the heavenly realms with every spiritual blessing in Christ (Ephesians 1:3).*

> *And God raised us up with Christ and seated us with him in the heavenly realms in Christ Jesus (Ephesians 2:6).*

Praying to God in order TO BE BLESSED or fighting the enemy in order TO BE BLESSED, because we see him as the obstructer of our progress, peace, health or wellbeing is not effective. Instead, we need to learn to already see ourselves in our spiritual position, namely, in the abundant life offered by Christ that comes with no sickness, no poverty or lack.

From childhood, we have been trained to fight for everything. In Christ, we need to train ourselves to receive what God has already released to meet our every need. Our circumstances can change when we align our views to the fact that being seated in Christ above all principalities and authorities that rule in the heavenlies is the greatest strategy God has set up for us to be able to have a mindset of victory.

So, once again, the strategy was finalised by God Himself when He seated us with Christ at His right hand. And this should enable each one of us to engage in any spiritual fight in the position of the giant fighting a grasshopper. Therefore, stop making evil powers bigger than they are. Stop magnifying the devil's power. Exalt the name of Jesus above every situation you are going through. Then, instead of praying to win our present battles, we actually need to claim the victory won by Christ for us. To be clear, all we need to do is to believe we are victorious in Christ:

> *Then Jesus said, "Did I not tell you that if you believe, you will see the glory of God?" (John 11:40).*

Does it not sound like our victory is expressed through our faith? Yes, it does! So, when praying strategically to claim our victory in the areas the enemy has been operating in our lives, we do not ask God to give us victory once again… we should ask Him to bring us into unity with Christ. When that happens, the circumstances or situations we are fighting may still be visible, but they will not undermine our relationship with the Lord, and our faith will remain strong enough to lead us to reject and refute unbelief or defeat. Then, we can take back control of the situation, and exercise the rule and reign planned by God when He seated us on His throne of grace with Christ.

Maybe, reading this part, you expected to learn about a supernatural strategy that would enable you to gain your battles. All strategies elaborated by God are effective when applied. And the truth is that, for our battles to be won, we need to stop fighting aimlessly, throwing ourselves into endless prayer and fasting as a religious exercise without believing in them. How many times have we heard people saying they are praying for a situation, but... But what? That added 'but' just negates your prayer... If you pray, then pray! If you fast, fast! And only believe, for all things are possible with God when we believe: *"Jesus said, 'Did I not tell you that if you believe, you will see the glory of God?'" (John 11:40)*. So, believe in your victory in Christ, receive that victory in faith in order to rule and exercise your authority from the seat of Christ.

Below is a discussion of two types of prayers we normally pray.

Maintenance Prayers

A maintenance prayer is the kind of prayer we do every day to keep our relationship with God real. He is our Father in Heaven, and just as Jesus spent time speaking to Him, we should, as His children, speak to Him all the time. Imagine a house where a loving father lives with his children but they speak to him only once a day, or only when they are in trouble. That would certainly show anyone who sees them the state of their relationship.

Confessing to be a child of God does not automatically mean you have a relationship with Him. How often, in a day, do you speak to God compared to someone you love (a parent, a spouse, a friend, your child)? Some people even find time to quarrel more with an adversary than they spend time talking to God. The lack of maintenance prayer reveals a misconception of who God is. That is why it is very surprising to hear about the number of people who 'hear' from God but are still so confused about what to do, or what direction to take. Can God truly speak to us while we are distracted? Well, maintenance prayers aim at improving our relationship with God and they are not crisis prayers.

Crisis Prayers

The Bible vividly illustrates crisis prayers through a number of men and women. Through Hannah who desperately cried for a child and ended up getting her answer. Through Jacob who fought all night with the Angel of God for his blessings and got his answer. Through Esther who proclaimed a corporate fast among the Jews when threatened with annihilation and got her answer.

These examples alone are enough for us to understand that, when we are facing a crisis, we have to change our way of praying right away. It's not the length of the prayer that matters but the fact that we acknowledge that our daily maintenance prayer needs to be taken to another level to be able to touch Heaven.

It would be very presumptuous to assert that we lack faith in God when facing a crisis. However, the lack of consistency in our prayer life can be the deciding factor in those moments: nobody can become a prayer warrior overnight. Someone who never fasted cannot start fasting and sustain that fasting properly overnight; someone who never prayed a whole night cannot stay up praying until morning. Nevertheless, when crises arise, we need to step up to pray an intense prayer until we get our answer. Hannah did not stop nor was she discouraged until she got her answer. Likewise, for Jacob, it took all night, for Esther three days. Though we are not told how long Hannah prayed, all we know is that she was constantly seeking God, crying out to Him. This teaches us that in times of crises, time is not relevant. Just keep crying out to God until He answers. For He will surely answer, the Bible assures us (Matthew 7:7).

Key to opening the lock

Every key is made to match and be compatible with a certain lock. The Concise Oxford English Dictionary defines a key as *"a small piece of shaped metal with incisions cut to fit the wards of a particular lock, which is inserted into a lock and turned to open or close it"*. Jesus said: *"And I will do whatever you ask in my name, so that the Father may be glorified in the Son. You may ask me for anything **in my name**, and I will do it"* *(John 14:13-14, emphasis added)*. Let's break this verse down to understand what the Lord is telling us: every day, we open and lock the doors of our homes. As soon as we put the key into the keyhole, we can operate it as we wish (open or close the door). The agent, or the main resource we use to activate the key in the keyhole, is our hand! Similarly, the key to open spiritual doors is given to us freely. Invoking the name of Jesus is one key to solving every problem we may face on earth because it has great power. This name was entrusted to the Church to use and should not be taken for granted: healing takes place in His name (Acts 3:6); evil spirits are powerless when we call on Jesus' name (Acts 16:16-21); demons are cast out by His name (Mark 16:17-18). Indeed, praying in Jesus' name is a promise Jesus gave us:

> *"And I will do whatever you ask in my name, so that the Father may be glorified in the Son. You may ask me for anything in my name, and I will do it"* *(John 14:13-14).*

Trusting in the name of Jesus should not be limited only to our ministries as the Bible adds that: *"And whatever you do, whether in word or deed, do it all in the name of the Lord Jesus, giving thanks to God the Father through him"* (Colossians 3:17).

Proverbs 18:10 says, *"The name of the Lord is a fortified tower; the righteous run to it and are safe."* In other words, it protects us from problems, dangers and difficulties. The Bible also says, *"The prayer of a righteous person is powerful and effective" (James 5:16).* The curious thing about this verse is that most of the time, we use it in isolation. In fact, this verse cannot be separated from the preceding one for all to make sense, because for our prayers to be *powerful and effective*, we are urged to ensure that we have not forsaken the name of Jesus by sinning. Look at what the whole verse says:

> *Therefore, confess your sins to each other and pray for each other so that you may be healed. The prayer of a righteous person is powerful and effective (James 5:16).*

Using this name, therefore means we have realised that our own name is powerless. Therefore, there must be special attention and expectation as we acknowledge that the name of Jesus that is used has authority and power in it. How can any authority be effective if those using it are not submitting to it in the first place?

One day, I was driving and came near a traffic jam. As I was stopped, I took my phone to call someone but placed it on my lap. A man on a motorbike stopped near my car and was staring at me... I was wondering why he looked so insistent, but I decided to ignore him and carried on with my phone call. When the traffic resumed a bit, I moved my car not paying attention to the man. To my surprise, I saw another motorbike stopping near my car, but this time, it was a police officer in full uniform who said: *"My colleague just saw you using your phone while driving; at the next turn, stop your car."* I was now escorted by both police officers, one in plain clothes and the other one in full uniform. Trust me, as much as I did not care about the one who did not wear his police uniform, when I saw the other one... the first thing I thought was: 'Caught in the act!' That is how we should react when using the name of Jesus when submitted to it. We can't just recite it because we have been taught to pray 'in Jesus' name'. The faith, submission, expectation and acknowledgement we have in this name is what makes us identify with it. In simple terms, this means we need to ensure that the things we are asking God for are things Jesus can pray about, so when we use His name, He can validate our prayers.

This brings us to this question: can anyone be effective using the name of Jesus while constantly playing in the devil's playground? Some Christians take the name and the blood of Jesus like that water we shower in after falling in the mud. This is not being submitted to Jesus! For the name of Jesus to be effective, we need to remain in the position that name has put us in: *"But you were **washed**, you were **sanctified**, you were **justified** in the name of the Lord Jesus Christ and by the Spirit of our God" (1 Corinthians*

6:11, emphasis added). Yes, washed, sanctified and justified, that is the position we should strive to maintain so our key, the name of Jesus, will be powerful and effective in our mouth.

Understanding spiritual authority

'God is good', 'God will do it', 'God will answer', can be considered platitudes that many believers mouth all the time. I say platitudes because they do this as a reflex action without attaching their faith to it. Sometimes God wants us to stand and see the work done but very often, we have to actively partner with Him to see results. God did not give Gideon victory without him raising an army to fight the enemy, as we demonstrated above. The same God did not give Jesus victory without Jesus bearing the pain on the cross first. God acts when we do our part of the battle in prayer, fasting, seeking His face and exercising the authority He has entrusted to us through Jesus to succeed in our mission. This is the first thing to understand about the spiritual authority given to us: it is for every believer, not only for those in leadership positions such as pastors, evangelists and prophets. As long as you are a believer of Jesus and you are walking towards heaven, His authority is for you to use. What is that authority?

> *"I have given you authority to trample on snakes and scorpions and to overcome all the power of the enemy; nothing will harm you" (Luke 10:19).*

Now, it would be very inappropriate to think that, because the authority was given to the believers, everyone can use it. Let me clarify this by a trivial example: a teenager who cannot drive a car may be offered a car. What will happen if this teenager starts off the car with the key they are offered? The answer is obvious: they are likely to kill someone or get killed. But does that mean the car is not theirs? Yes, they possess the car, but they will first need to learn to drive, get their driving licence and then practise driving safely and confidently.

Many people, especially sceptics, are tempted to apply the Scriptures in the way that suits them. Because the thirst for spiritual knowledge and experience is so widespread, they have neglected a key aspect of the spiritual authority we have in Christ. That is, developing an intimate relationship with the Lord. Let's put it this way: Jesus is the One giving us the authority and adds that our spiritual authority is not an end in itself. The end is to focus on what is happening in heaven: *"Nevertheless, do not rejoice that the spirits submit to you, but rejoice that your names are written in heaven" (Luke 10:20)*.

Today, many servants of God have misused the spiritual authority given by the Lord and use it as merchandise for crowd attraction and material gain. Likewise, many believers have exalted those ministers who display spectacular spiritual gifts, instead of setting their eyes on Jesus without whom we can do absolutely nothing (John 15:5).

This brings us to the point that spiritual authority is a means given to the Church to fulfil the plan of God and to establish His rulership on earth. So, for us to use this authority, we must remember that it works alongside obedience and submission to the Word, the authorities and the institutions. God has established on earth. In today's society, people who rebel against the authorities are seen as heroes and children have been taught that, growing up, all that matters, are their own feelings, their wants and their personal boundaries. Many people come to church with the same mindset, looking only for their own happiness and throwing away principles they consider as limitations or a source of external control. Yet, they know by heart the verse that tells them they have spiritual authority, and they want to exercise it. How many people have left a church because they were told they are not ready to do what they wanted to do?

Understanding the reason **for our spiritual authority**

Understanding why God has given us authority is indispensable.

> *You have made them a little lower than the angels and crowned them with glory and honor. You made them rulers over the works of your hands; you put everything under their feet (Psalm 8:5-6).*

We are supposed to rule over the works of God's hands, and everything is already put at our disposal for that purpose. Now, you may ask: 'How come I don't feel like everything is under my feet right now?' The answer is the fact that you may not have identified the area to exercise your spiritual authority yet, which therefore means you may be exercising it in a place where God has not (or has not yet) assigned you to operate. Let's look at what Apostle Paul says:

> *Neither do we go beyond our limits by boasting of work done by others. Our hope is that, as your faith continues to grow, our sphere of activity among you will greatly expand (2 Corinthians 10:15).*

Many people confuse their position in church with their ministry: being a pastor does not necessarily give you the gift to operate miracles. Through your preaching, God can work miracles without you having to organise a specific deliverance crusade. That is alluded to by Apostle Paul in the above verse as he is showing us he was aware of his sphere of authority and he tried not to go beyond it. Once we go beyond our spiritual territory, we open the way for evil spirits to deceive us, operate and make us believe that God is working in us and through us. The work is vast and with few workers in the field, so why would God want everybody in a local church to become a pastor, a healing minister, a prophet? The sad truth is, if you don't know the limits of your spiritual territory, you cannot rule over anything effectively.

Again, many people speak out there, 'This is the message from God,' 'God said…' sincerely believing that what they say comes from God. Yet, there is a problem when a 'divine' message does not line up with the Word of God, is self-centred or condemning of others. God never started using anybody in the Word of God to minister to others without first using them to minister to themselves, because the first spiritual territory we must deal with is our minds! Before ministering to (not to mention criticising) anyone, have you already demolished arguments and every pretension that sets itself up against the knowledge of God, and taken captive each of your thoughts to make them obedient to Christ (2 Corinthians 10:5)?

Preparing and equipping

Being called by Christ an ambassador of the Kingdom does not make you one if you don't submit to Him: there are some terrorists who choose to kill their fellow citizens because of their rebellious hearts. That is the reason why, before a believer starts operating in any ministry, the need for preparation is unavoidable:

> *So, Christ himself gave the apostles, the prophets, the evangelists, the pastors and teachers, to equip his people for works of service, so that the body of Christ may be built up (Ephesians 4:11-12).*

This is clear: whoever operates out of this framework has not been authorised because there is a breach in the spiritual order of things. A child is born on earth out of parents. In the same way, Christ has not allowed anyone to claim that the Spirit of God has equipped them, skipping the Scripture above. Let's even go further here: Christ was baptised by a man, John the Baptist *"to fulfill all righteousness" (Matthew 3:15)*. Did Jesus need to be baptised by a mere human being? Even Apostle Paul traces back the places he was trained, before being equipped directly by the Lord Himself (Galatians 1:12). We learn more in the verse below:

> *I am a Jew, born in Tarsus of Cilicia, but brought up in this city. I studied under Gamaliel and was thoroughly trained in the law of our ancestors. I was just as zealous for God as any of you are today (Acts 22:3).*

This leads us to the twelve disciples who sat at the feet of the Master for three years before being sent out into the field.

Indeed, preparation is essential for every believer who wants to serve God: when we first start following Jesus, we all are believers. Through training, we become Christians as our actions and lifestyle start showing we are being crucified and no longer led by our fleshly lusts. Now, there is a further stage that requires abandoning the world and being set apart for service. That is when we become disciples. The problem is that some mere believers try to exercise the authority that only a disciple is capable of. Doing so is dangerous as it is like a primary or secondary school student trying to behave as a university student when facing a problem. The lack of training, experience and knowledge might just lead that tenderfoot into problems out of their depth to handle.

So, if you have not moved your state of service to Jesus from a mere follower to a disciple, how do you expect to deal with principalities and spiritual authorities? Let's remember that, the spiritual realm is highly organised. So, must we. Grace has not dismantled the established order of authority. That is why God the Son submitted to the will of God the Father, and today, God the Spirit is operating because God the Son asked God the Father to send Him. Yes, order matters for God. Not submitting to orders disqualifies us for great service for the Kingdom because God will not risk putting any of His children in danger. Yet, we expose ourselves by wanting to serve and operate when still unequipped and unprepared, not to say uncrucified.

Exercise your spiritual authority

To be able to exercise our authority, we first need to know who we are in Christ. Our authority has been established from the throne of God. In other words, it comes from our spiritual position in Heaven, seated with Christ at the right hand of the Father (Ephesians 1:20-21). But this is not enough. Being seating in Heaven does not remove us from the earth where we are still walking physically. And that implies that we are still submitted to the natural laws of this earth, so we need to develop intimacy with the Lord to distinctly hear His voice. The reason submission comes before hearing from God is that, if we don't learn to submit to God and He starts talking to us, we might start reasoning with Him, or disobey, or worse, mistake the Lord's voice for our own voice or the devil's voice. Jesus did not start giving revelations to Saul on the road to Damascus: He simply stopped him on his way to sin, blinded him physically, and then sent Ananias to validate Saul's calling.

> *Then Ananias went to the house and entered it. Placing his hands on Saul, he said, "Brother Saul, the Lord – Jesus, who appeared to you on the road as you were coming here – has sent me so that you may see again and be filled with the Holy Spirit." Immediately, something like scales fell from Saul's eyes, and he could see again. He got up and was baptized, and after taking some food, he regained his strength (Acts 9:17-19).*

Once again, Jesus who established His church follows the order He has set for the validation of a calling. It was done through one of His many disciples, Ananias, who obeyed the Lord despite his hesitation to go to Saul because of his notoriety. We also understand through Ananias that the Lord wants us to be humble and truthful enough to obey Him despite our opinions or feelings to the contrary. Then He will instruct us with what to do and say for His purposes to be fulfilled. That is the first stage of exercising our spiritual authority. Indeed, it is to Ananias that the Lord revealed what He was going to do with Saul:

And not only that, God used Ananias to heal Paul (Acts 9:17). Ananias was instructed to exercise his authority, knowing what the Lord wanted to accomplish. Because he had been commissioned directly by Jesus, he was acting in the name of Jesus. All that he declared worked as the Lord had instructed him.

Today, we have the same authority that was entrusted to Ananias and we are expected by the Lord to succeed whenever we use His name. Now, how much faith do we need to empower the words we speak when operating in the name of Jesus? The fact is, our authority works in accordance with our faith:

"Have faith in God," Jesus answered. "Truly I tell you, if anyone says to this mountain, 'Go, throw yourself into the sea,' and does not doubt in their heart but believes that what they say will happen, it will be done for them. Therefore, I tell you, whatever you ask for in prayer, believe that you have received it, and it will be yours" (Mark 11:22-24).

"Not doubt in their heart!" We sometimes pray in the name of Jesus, but nothing happens because of our doubts. Maybe we should, just like Ananias, first become the Lord's witnesses. What characterised all the disciples was the fact that they were true witnesses. Today, we want to be doers of Jesus' miracles. No, He

is the miracle-doer and we must tell the world what He has done and is doing. That's what witnesses do.

If we want our spiritual authority to work powerfully and effectively, we need to remember the words of Ananias to Apostle Paul:

> *"Then he said: 'The God of our ancestors has chosen you to know his will and to see the Righteous One and to hear words from his mouth. You will be his witness to all people of what you have seen and heard'" (Acts 22:14-15).*

Being witnesses means we are not active in the scene, though we are chosen to be witnesses. So, instead of going to look for work to do, why not let God go ahead of us and tell us: *"I am sending someone to pray for so that they may be healed."* The problem is that we are not always focused enough to hear God speak to us or guide us, so we lead the show instead. This limits the action of the Holy Spirit.

At the very start of my ministry, I used to write daily meditations that I posted on Facebook. One night, I was praying, and it was around 2.00 am. The Lord said to me, 'On Sunday, I am sending you someone to pray for and they shall be healed.' I wrote this message in a notebook because I used to record all the messages I got from the Lord as I was still learning to hear His voice. In the morning, I showed my son the notes, saying, 'The Lord said He was going to send someone to church. I will pray for the person and the person will be healed.' When Sunday came, I was expectant. But nobody new came to church that day. I really felt disappointed and thought maybe that was not the voice of the Lord, but mine.

Later that afternoon, a young man contacted me after reading the meditation I had posted on Facebook for that Sunday morning. His questions were a bit annoying as they were personal, so I dropped the conversation. Three hours later, around 5.00 pm, the same young man started a conversation again. I told him I would answer Him only if what he was asking me was related to the Bible. He asked me if in our organisation we produced medicine. I told him we were a church, and we pray to the Healer who produces the medicine that never fails to heal. Then he told me that he was only 30 years old and he had kidney stones. I suggested we pray; then I asked him if he could fast. He said he could not. So, I offered to fast on his behalf, and we were going to pray. I asked him to send me his phone number so I could call him for prayer. As he lived in Qatar, I told him I was going to call him the following day because I needed to buy a phone card to call Qatar! After, this conversation, I told my son this man was most likely the one God said He was going to send for me to pray for.

The following day, I started fasting before I prayed on the phone at the set time together with the young man. We prayed for three days. Then we stopped because he had to travel to Bangladesh for his scheduled surgery. About ten days after our last prayer, I saw a missed call from a foreign number; obviously, it was him calling from Bangladesh this time. When I called the number back, this young man was praising the Lord saying that he had gone for surgery. When they did a pre-surgery examination, they found that the kidney stones were dissolving, so he no longer needed surgery. All glory to Jesus! I cannot tell you the joy felt on both sides for what God had done. The funny part of the story is that this young man started giving my contact details to friends, who wanted me to pray for them for money issues, business issues, everything! But I told them that I had finished my divine assignment and they should seek their own pastors for prayer.

To wrap up, witnessing for Christ is the key to exercising our spiritual authority. Peter, Ananias and Paul show us that revelation through the Word of God, boldness, active faith and humility are the main qualities of overcomers and achievers in God's Kingdom.

Chapter VII
The Mystery of the Upper Room

Creating your upper room

The Christian life is a constant fight against the enemy, and our greatest weapons remain obedience to and application of the Word. It is easier to pray in a place where we are visible and can be encouraged by others. That is why so many believers have a surge of emotional (rather than spiritual) reactions when they attend a church service. Togetherness is good, but also there is a need to learn, even discipline ourselves, to pray on our own regularly. *"But when you pray, **go into your room, close the door and pray** to your Father, who is unseen. Then your Father, who sees what is done in secret, will reward you" (Matthew 6:6, emphasis added).*

This is creating an upper room, a place where you regularly meet with your Heavenly Father. This place can be anywhere you are comfortable to pray: at home, in a park, even simply in your car or in a designated place of prayer. The most important thing is that this place is dedicated for you to stand before the presence of the Lord.

The Lord is everywhere, and He sees all our actions. When we decide to come into His presence, we express our intentional step to turn to Him in prayer, thanksgiving, devotion or simply reading His Word. He discerns our intention to be alone with Him; thus, He establishes a spiritual relationship with us that can result in the inner witness of His Spirit that dwells within us. That's what we call entering the upper room! All great servants of God, including Jesus, had an upper room. For example, Jesus' upper room was in a secluded place, most often in the desert or on a mountain:

> *But Jesus often withdrew to lonely places and prayed (Luke 5:16).*
>
> *One of those days Jesus went out to a mountainside to pray, and spent the night praying to God (Luke 6:12).*
>
> *After he had dismissed them, he went up on a mountainside by himself to pray. Later that night, he was there alone (Matthew 14:23).*

Every child of God and disciple of Christ must develop a personal relationship or communion with the Lord. This time of solitude in the presence of God is vital and must come before any public action. Acts 6:4 shows that the apostles took time in prayer before preaching and, from Genesis to Revelation, we can observe that all the men and women that God used powerfully were devoted to prayer.

The prophet's upper room

Too often, we consider the gift of prophecy only as a sudden inspiration that occurs during a worship service or an assembly of believers. Yet, spiritual preparation, created by the time spent alone with the Lord, is needed if we want this gift to manifest in our daily fellowship with the Lord. That is what allows our hearts to become more sensitive to the voice of the Holy Spirit. In other words, when a servant of God gives a prophetic message, they are only conveying audibly what God wants to communicate. But there is the hidden part to it, which is, in fact, the time the messenger spends with God in the secret of their room. This is the most important part of prophecy.

Once, I was at home with friends and I decided to go to bed. Once in my bed, I had already switched the light off after my prayer. I stood up to put on the light again. One of my friends heard me and asked me if I was not sleeping yet. I replied that I needed to pray for a sister from our church because I had just received a prompting in my spirit to do so. So, I prayed for the sister. The next morning, around 8.00 am, the sister called me asking for prayer. I said, 'Everything is well; the Lord made your prayer request to me last night.' Praise the Lord!

During another private time, God once told me to call a sister (giving me her name) and tell her to position herself well because He was going to bless her. As I was going to see the sister the next day, I thought to myself, I would just wait until tomorrow. About 30 minutes later, this sister called saying, 'Pastor, I don't know why I am calling you, but I just wanted to call…' I laughed and replied, 'I know why you are calling me. The Lord just told me to tell you to position yourself; He will bless you.' Then we discussed a bit about how she should position herself. Two days later, this sister received a phone call from a big company that offered her a life-changing position accompanied by a brand-new car... and she has been working there for four years. Praise the Lord!

Indeed, the prophet who speaks on behalf of God must live most of his life immersed in God's presence and say as Elijah did, *"I swear by the Lord Almighty, in whose presence I stand"* (1 Kings 18:15 NLT).

In conclusion, if you want to be led by the Spirit of God, it is necessary to develop spiritual sensitivity. This cannot be done in a group setting such as a church service, while so many things happen according to a set schedule. Thus, creating an upper room allows you to have a place of encounter and intimacy in the presence of the Almighty God, your Heavenly Father. There, we come not only to pray, praise and worship the Lord, but also to quietly sit in the presence of God, to listen to His voice, and hear His Word. It is a place where God speaks to us, revealing His thoughts and purposes to us.

Chapter VIII
Willing, Available, Ready?

Many believers trust Jesus as their Lord and Saviour, but very few people trust in the Redeemer. Yet, they are professing Christians. It's important to emphasize that saying we are willing to serve the Lord does not necessarily make us available or ready to do so, for biblical Christians are only those who do the will of God. Barnabas and Saul (Paul) taught many people in Antioch for about a year: some were disciples, but, in general, they were called 'Christians' or 'little Christs' (Acts 11:26).

The makings of a disciple

Today, the name 'Christian' can now be considered a general term for all those who accept the Lordship of Jesus but have not yet made Him their Master. In fact, disciples of Christ know what a crucified life is, and the Lord empowers them on missions to do great things. Elisha is a good example of a disciple. He faithfully followed his master Elijah while serving God and was able to do much greater miracles than Elijah.

If a census were taken in your church today, could you categorically state whether you are a Christian or a disciple? The disciples learned from Jesus and had to be stripped of their own weaknesses, fears, doubts and pride before they could start serving with boldness. Even Apostle Paul, though most of what He received was through revelation from Jesus Christ (Galatians 1:11-12), spent three years quietly in Arabia (Galatians 1:17-18) before going to Jerusalem to minister.

Indeed, every new believer should learn to be silent, accept to remain under instruction for at least three years, while bathing in the Word of God and building up their faith. Many believers keep failing to win all battles because they have neglected to first check their spiritual barometer. They may be trying to operate spiritually in areas they cannot handle yet. Establish your spiritual position before you can consider fighting! Nobody plays a video game from level two without completing level one. Deal with your own fears and limitations, before you attempt to cast out demons for others. That's one basic secret to true spiritual breakthrough. In doing so, you will also learn to thank God instead of murmuring about what is wrong in your life. You cannot go further with the Lord without first learning *"the secret of being content in any and every situation, whether well fed or hungry, whether living in plenty or in want"* *(Philippians 4:12).*

What also leads many to easily fall into the routine of complaining is the Martha attitude: they are still not spiritually strong but want to be involved in spiritual matters. The fact is, just like Martha, everyone who complains in church has not yet understood Christianity or the Church of Christ, which is faith centred in Christ, not on faith based on works. The time has come for you to get ready to move on. To be ready, do not count on anyone but on yourself, for this is part of the covenant of grace through Christ.

Be willing

In 1 Chronicles 29:5, King David asked the people an important question we should ask ourselves today: *"Now, who is willing to consecrate themselves to the Lord today?"*

Willing means being delighted to do something. Unless we are naturally disposed to evil, our willingness to serve is normally motivated by very good intentions. The Bible even tells us many times that God wants us to serve Him wholeheartedly. This is to say God wants our motive for serving Him to be love above anything else. We should then understand that when we serve God, who is invisible, we often do it through people who are visible. And it is very important to insist on this because some people would say, 'I am here for God…' or 'I am doing this for God' when they imply they don't want to have anything to do with anyone… in the house of God. Yet, we read that *"Whoever claims to love God yet hates a brother or sister is a liar. For whoever does not love their brother and sister, whom they have seen, cannot love God, whom they have not seen"* (1 John 4:20).

When we are led by ingratitude, rebellion or even selfishness, we cannot be willing to serve, as it would not be aligned with God's Word. Let's recall that the Spirit is always willing, but our flesh is weak (see Matthew 26:41). So, when we are willing to serve, we should do it in a pure spirit for our service to be honourable and acceptable before God, knowing that willing service leads to the fulfilment of the plans of God:

> *For if the willingness is there, the gift is acceptable according to what one has, not according to what one does not have (2 Corinthians 8:12).*

This makes it clear that being willing is important because God uses only willing hearts. He does not want to create robots. He wants an army of willing children who do not feel compelled to serve, to go to church or to love one another. He does not look at our background to use us. The Bible says:

> *But the LORD said to Samuel, "Do not consider his appearance or his height, for I have rejected him. The Lord does not look at the things people look at. People look at the outward appearance, but the Lord looks at the heart" (1 Samuel 16:7).*

Definitely, it is what He finds in our hearts that matters to Him. He calls those willing, not those who are necessarily able: Moses, king Josiah, king David, Jeremiah, Apostle Paul... all these characters and many more would not qualify for service before man, but their willing hearts to do the will of God made the difference. Does that mean they did not object to taking up the missions God had assigned them? No! Moses saw his stuttering as an impediment, but God said, *"I will help you speak and will teach you what to say" (Exodus 4:12)*. You don't need to be super educated or have great possessions or abilities to serve the Lord. He is searching our hearts every day. Has He already found the selfless willingness to serve Him in it? Or is He still waiting for you to be willing on His terms and not your worldly terms to be able to assign you a mission? When it comes to being willing, it depends on us and it is entirely our decision. God has great plans for each one of us, but only those who are willing to serve Him wholeheartedly are the ones He sends. As for the others, He continues to wait until they make the voluntary decision to abandon themselves to His will.

Be available

The fact is, being willing is key to winning the battle of your life. But that is still not enough. Many people who are sick, pray to God but they are not willing to believe in more than what they have settled for in their minds. God can work in a way you may have never thought of! Maybe we are too used to doing things our way and have never wondered why the results are delayed. Maybe also, the time has come to turn your dormant faith into active faith and allow the Spirit of God, your Helper, to take over.

The same, for reasons of their own, many people refuse to go to church and say they are praying at home. Good! Stay home while the Bible teaches us that God's presence is in the assembly (see Hebrews 10:25). Let me remind you that when king Jehoshaphat heard that three armies were coming against him and his people, he went to cry out to God… in the Temple… and there, God told him through the prophet not to worry, He would give them victory and fight the battle on their behalf (see 2 Chronicles 20:1-22).

A woman had an issue of blood. She heard Jesus was coming to town. Even though she was considered unclean and prohibited from touching people, she took the risk of being stoned to be able to touch Jesus (see Luke 8:43-48). As soon as she touched Jesus, a power left Him, and she was healed. Isolating yourself from others, especially when you are in trouble, IS NOT OF God! Also, know that in Heaven, there is togetherness, and it is on earth we start our eternity: you can't avoid the Church of Christ, but claim that He is using you: *"How good and pleasant it is when God's people live together in unity" (Psalm 133:1).*

Let's also remember that Jesus said when two or three gather in His name, there He is in the midst of us. So why do you think that you can have healing, restoration and wholeness again by yourself or on your own terms and conditions? We all know that misuse of any medication can create an adverse effect in our body. Don't we consider that the misapplication of the Word of God can also create adverse spiritual conditions in our lives? If we don't use the right ingredients for God's promises, we can't expect God's hand to move. For example, God has already released blessing, healing and abundant grace to impact our lives; however, they sometimes don't manifest because we are not prepared to change our mindsets.

The Word of God is all about Jesus transforming lives. Every day, we hear or say words of condemnation of ourselves or others. The amount of negativity we speak about ourselves is sometimes greater than what others say about us. If we do not go deeply into the Word of God but always remain shallow in our understanding, our actions and our bad habits will never be transformed. In the end, we will suffer the consequences of those bad habits.

Be ready

If being willing is a matter of looking at what we want and aligning ourselves with the Word, being available is doing everything that God says to do in His Word, for example, fasting, praying, going to church. Now, the greatest difficulty is being ready! Let's look into the Word:

> *As Jesus started on His way, a man ran up to him and fell on his knees before Him.*
> *"Good teacher," he asked, "what must I do to inherit eternal life?"*
> *"Why do you call me good?" Jesus answered. "No one is good—except God alone. You know the commandments: 'You shall not murder, you shall not commit adultery, you*

*shall not steal, you shall not give false testimony, you shall
not defraud, honor your father and mother.'"
"Teacher," he declared, "all these I have kept since I was
a boy."
Jesus looked at him and loved him. "One thing you lack,"
he said. "Go, sell everything you have and give to the poor,
and you will have treasure in heaven. Then come, follow
me."
At this the man's face fell. He went away sad, because he
had great wealth (Mark 10:17-22).*

Aren't we very often like this man? We have an idea of what to do to get something from God, but we never really expect God to ask something of us. The young man was WILLING to follow Jesus and he made himself AVAILABLE by reaching out to the Lord. He thought He was READY – until the Lord told him one thing he lacked. Let me ask you candidly:

- What is the one thing that is hindering your walk with the Lord?

- What is the one thing you lack for your healing?

- What is the one thing the Lord has asked you to abandon?

Don't end up feeling torn and sad like the young rich man! He was too proud to abandon the one thing that gave him security: his wealth. We can claim we are humble; we can behave humbly, dress humbly... but true humility is doing what God tells us to do! How many have left church because they were told something they did not want to hear or did not like? But the same people will stay at their workplace even after being corrected or instructed to do something they did not like.

At the start of my ministry, I invested time and money in souls who never stayed in church. I was discouraged until I understood that people have many motives for seeking God: many came to church only to be prayed for and nothing else. I did not know, but God knew. Others attended service expecting a miracle that day... but did not see anything and never came back. Some others, touristic Christians, hop from church to church convinced they are filled with the Holy Spirit and want to teach people how to be good Christians. When the Lord opened my eyes to understand that the heart of man is not to be trusted, I stopped trying to 'keep' people in the church. Instead, I started teaching them to know Christ.

By the grace of God, I have travelled a lot to preach the Word and met many people from different cultures. Apart from finding the same traits of Christian character across the board, I have observed that people always defend their Christian practices based on their background or their culture, which is mainly influenced by the rules of man. When you or any other Christian start justifying practices which do not conform to biblical Christianity, can you say your will is submitted to God?

Know that Satan is defeated

Before accepting Christ, most people lived an up-and-down life, not questioning the activities of the devil in their own lives. Now, once they pick up some Bible verses, they want to start casting out demons. This is a sure recipe for defeat, hardly for a victorious life. We need to remember that God cast the devil out of Heaven long before He created man. When God created man, He wanted us to enforce His rule on earth to show Satan that his power has been wrested from him. Jesus came to take back what the devil had stolen from Adam and Eve.

In light of this, it is perplexing that today's church is preoccupied with fighting the devil through constant spiritual warfare. Yes, we are at war with Satan and his hierarchy of demons, but the greatest victory is to acknowledge that the devil is already defeated and should be left where God placed him: under our feet. Why then do we spend so much time casting out devils instead of proclaiming Jesus in our assemblies? When we walk, do we walk focusing on what is under our feet rather than on the horizon in front of us? If the today's church would stop its continuous involvement with evil spiritual activities and focus more on Christ's achievements on the Cross, more souls would be freed from oppression, and there would be greater victory. When we understand that, we should shift our worship to God alone, for He does not share His glory. He has already established rules for us to live victorious lives.

No weapon formed against us shall prosper

"Behold, I have created the craftsman who fans the coals into flame and forges a weapon fit for its task; and I have created the destroyer to wreak havoc. No weapon formed against you shall prosper, and you will refute every tongue that accuses you. This is the heritage of the LORD's servants, and their vindication is from Me," declares the LORD (Isaiah 54:16-17).

Obviously, there are many weapons that are formed against us in the spirit realm. Those weapons may target different areas of our lives and overwhelm, even paralyse, us. But in His Word, God says He is the One who *"created the craftsman who fans the coals into flame and forges a weapon fit for its task";* He also created *"the destroyer to wreak havoc" (Isaiah 54:16).* This means that every time we are attacked by demonic activity, these are only created entities who cannot defy their Creator. Moreover, God knows that He has already seated us in a place where we cannot be enslaved anymore (Ephesians 1:20-21).

Now, if God knows our situations and circumstances, why are we sometimes intimidated by the enemy? The answer is simple: our own fears and behaviours! Sometimes, the enemy has not even declared war on us but we are already reacting in anticipation, owing to our fears. The greatest stumbling block in man is fear. How many people run away at the sight of a dog? They don't know if the dog will bark and attack them, but they assume it will. They size up the situation themselves and, perceiving danger, they run.

Looking at things only from our perspective can prevent us from stepping out according to the promptings of the Holy Spirit.

Many people in the church don't want to change. They are used to doing things one way, so they expect the results to occur the way they have imagined. They are never happy with the outcome, so they complain. Then, when facing hardship, they parrot: *"no weapon formed against me shall prosper."*

As Christians, we should stop automatically reciting the Word of God, depriving it of its power. If we are quoting the Word and it means nothing to us, then it is in vain. Routine prayers don't fly beyond our roofs because, when we start praying as a routine, our minds are not even into recognising what we are asking God for, not to mention we ourselves not even believing in what we are praying. Calling on 'our Father in Heaven…' should encourage us to show great reverence to the Almighty, the Alpha and the Omega, the One and only One who can change our situation. Can you imagine yourself calling on the president of your country and not giving him all your attention or entertaining any thought but the fact that you are in the presence of that high authority? So why, do we stand before God centred on us instead of on Him and what He has to tell us?

God is in control of everything. He has already made provision for weapons formed against us not to prevail. So, despite what the craftsman is producing, despite what the destroyer is scheming,

God wants His children to focus on Him, the Mighty One. As we do so, then their weapons are neutralised. For our confession of the Word of God to produce fruit in our lives, we first need to know who God is and remember that He put His Word in our hearts, so we can do His will… the decision is ours. In the same way, do we focus more on the person who holds the weapon or on the weapons presenting themselves to us? Do we become paralysed instead of trusting that God, who is in control of everything, will deliver us from the paw of the lion and the bear?

Also, we pray that no weapon formed against us shall prosper when we feel like blocking an impending attack. Now, the knowledge of the Word and standing on the Word in faith are the two counter-offensives we are given to defeat the enemy's attempts. When God said, *"I am the Lord… no weapon formed against you shall prevail…"* His people were already under attack; it was not a warning about an attack. In the midst of that, God was reassuring His people of victory and inviting them to trust Him. So, when we are already in a battle, we should remember that we shall succeed anyway because no weapon shall prevail.

So, during our battles, let's learn to glorify God who has already given us victory because of what Christ did on the Cross. No matter what man says or how much darkness has surrounded you, you should remain confident that no weapon will prosper to put you down as long as you continue trusting in God. But, some of us may find it quite difficult to trust God in general because our minds are programmed and our experiences, our expectations, our backgrounds and our extensive knowledge are always blocking the door, preventing the Lord from entering our hearts and working out His plans.

If we fail to allow the Lord into our hearts, then we are exposing ourselves to many dangers. Let's first recall that there is no safe place in this world. Life is based on grace and we should be thankful always because we do not control anything. An unpleasant event can happen to any of us anywhere, from your bed to the street. So how do we protect ourselves against adversity or the world? As mentioned above, our attitude is critical when faced with misfortune. But, let's return to the Scriptures: *"If anyone does attack you, it will not be my doing; whoever attacks you will surrender to you" (Isaiah 54:15)*. This verse comes before God reminds us that He created the person who can create a weapon, so that weapon formed against us shall not prevail. In other words, God makes a way for victory for us before we go through hardships. It is our responsibility to identify that way by the means He offers us in the Scriptures: fellowship, praise and worship, prayer, fasting, the Word and the indwelling presence of the Spirit.

Discipline

Our churches don't stress the importance of self-discipline enough, and the enemy uses our lack of discipline to worsen our circumstances. As much as we claim that the weapons formed by the enemy are useless, we should also ensure we do things in order and in a way that God can intervene. Yes, setting priorities and self-discipline are keys to allow *"no weapon formed against you to prevail."* Let's say you started on a journey. On the journey, you meet someone going in the opposite direction. You know your destination is not theirs… but you cave in to their pressure and change your route. Have you noticed the invisible weapon that has just rerouted you from your initial destination? Maybe your blessing was exactly where you were heading. The devil, an imitator of God and a deceiver, will distract you just so that you don't get to where God wants you to be at the right time.

Discipline is a complex and sensitive topic as it is hard for believers to sometimes accept the idea of being disciplined in church. In fact, a Christian should be an example, especially for non-believers. Thus, we must walk according to the commandments of God and be guided by the Holy Spirit who is our light. Only the light in us enables the distinction between us and non-believers who, by contrast, tend to be more attached to the things of the world and do not value the principles of the Kingdom of God. Christian discipline is present when we are not following the pattern of this world but choose to do what is pleasing to God (Romans 12:2).

An example of not following the pattern of this world is to have an irreproachable course of action and to respect certain principles. This is where the concept of discipline comes in. But, how, in practice, does a child of God lead a disciplined life?

Many areas need disciplining and one of them should come first as it has the power to kill or produce life: our tongue! As Christians, we must always try to speak with wisdom, in other words, master the words coming out of our mouth. The Word of God is powerful. In the same way, a spoken word can have significant repercussions. Remember that *"The tongue has the power of life and death, and those who love it will eat its fruit"* (Proverbs 18:21). For this reason, we should not say negative words about ourselves, our loved ones, our work and so on. In addition, we must learn to discipline our ears: for instance, avoid participating in gossip or listening to secular music; and also ensure our eyes are not filled with lustful desires. Ultimately, a Christian must reflect the image of God.

We are the children of God. Everywhere we are, whether it be at work, at church or in the street, we must behave like ambassadors of Christ! This means, showing respect to their authorities, being on time as God is timely, manifesting love, forgiving and praying for their enemies and persecutors instead of cursing them. Besides, as our church is *the house of God*, we should be very careful not to allow our services to turn into entertainment, thus destroying the sacred nature of the church, a place where fellow believers meet to commune with God, share the Word and live out their faith corporately.

CONCLUSION

God is ready; but are we? We may think we are ready, but the truth is that we are so often just like the prodigal son who wasted his inheritance before the appointed time. God is not a man to be fooled: He knows our hearts and when we are truly ready and operational. He is not looking for theoreticians but for practitioners of His Word, for every promise of God is to be taken deeply because the Word of God is alive… 'How do I make it alive?'

Rest in the Word

Nobody has ever asked us to think through or over-analyse the Word of God. Maybe all you need to do now is to concentrate on the Word itself, knowing that the Word is the Lord Jesus. Let's make Jesus the centre of our walk by silencing all external noises that distract us from Him. It is not normal for a believer to be looking all over the place for guidance endlessly. This is a reflection of faith without the Word made flesh. In practice, when facing sickness, for instance, we know the Word of God says, *"But he was pierced for our transgressions, he was crushed for our iniquities; the punishment that brought us peace was on him, and by his wounds we are healed" (Isaiah 53:5)*. All we need to do then is to proclaim this verse, having in mind that the weapon (sickness) shall not prosper as we put all our trust in God, regardless of what the doctors say, or how things look. What makes the Word of God ineffective is the shallow use of God's promises, which nullifies the grace we have received in Christ to compensate for our weaknesses.

The Bible shows us that Satan knows the Scriptures and he used them to tempt Jesus. *"You believe that there is one God. Good! Even the demons believe that—and shudder" (James 2:19)*. So, what distinguishes us from the devil? The Love of God and the revelation that we have within us! This is to say that we need to incorporate the living Word of God for the Word to serve our interests. God gave us, as His children, the Word that He made alive for us not to be defeated but to handle the victory that Jesus dearly earned for us. In John 15:7, Jesus shows us how important the Word is to Him: *"If you remain in me and my words remain in you, ask whatever you wish, and it will be done for you."*

Why then, do we ask for things and not get them? Why do we claim the promises of God and not receive them? Are we not in Christ? Yes, we are, and we do abide in Him. So, what could be missing, then? THE WORD ABIDING IN US! A Word you receive that is inconsistent cannot benefit you, like a flickering light. The truth is that, most of the time, worldly reflexes (or human reactions) take precedence over the Word when specific challenges hit us.

Let us live the Word in all situations, especially in times of crisis. Let us do as Jesus did, who fulfilled the Word, using it even to the point of death. If we would apply the Word in all our circumstances, we will win the war of life.